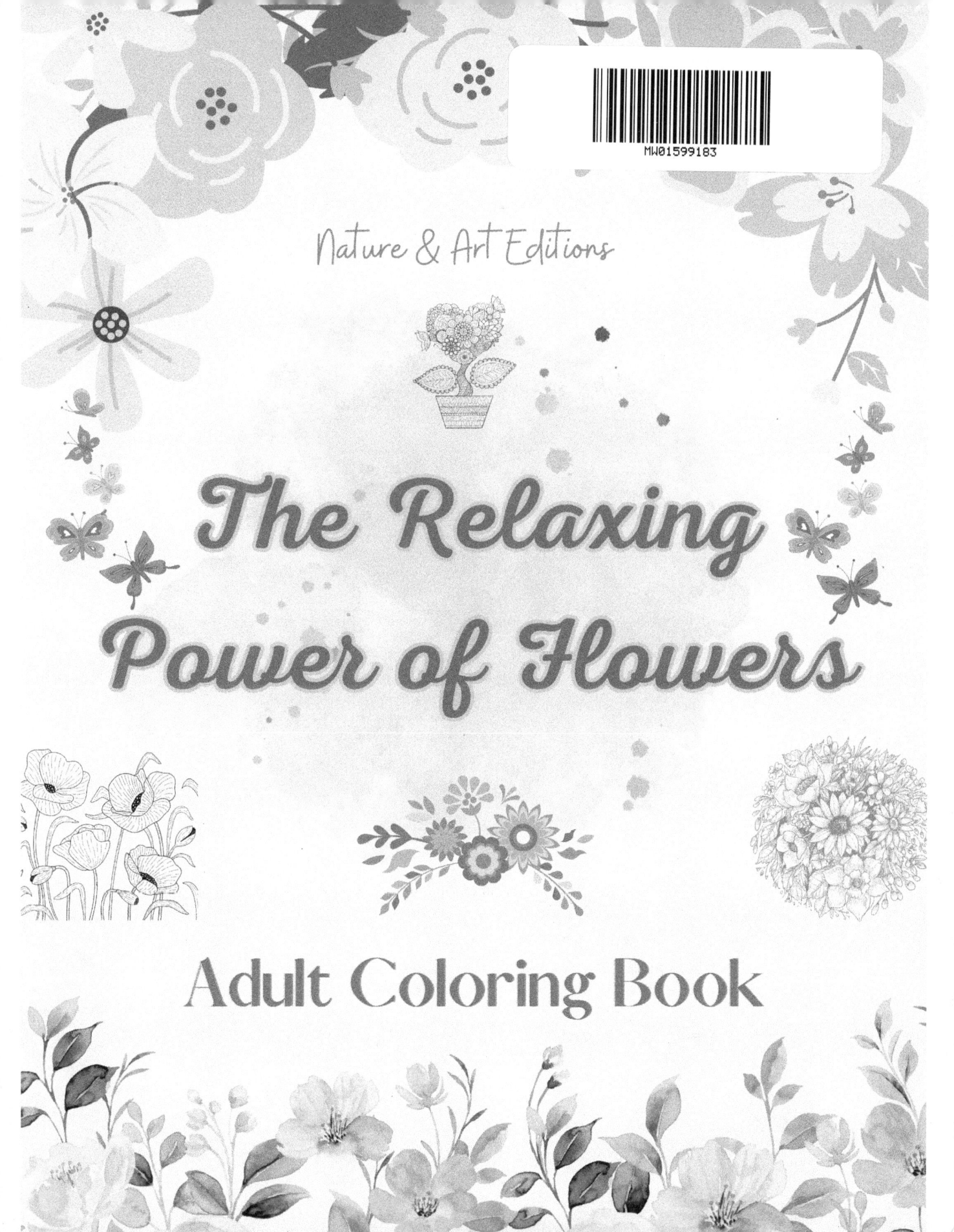

Nature & Art Editions

The Relaxing Power of Flowers

Adult Coloring Book

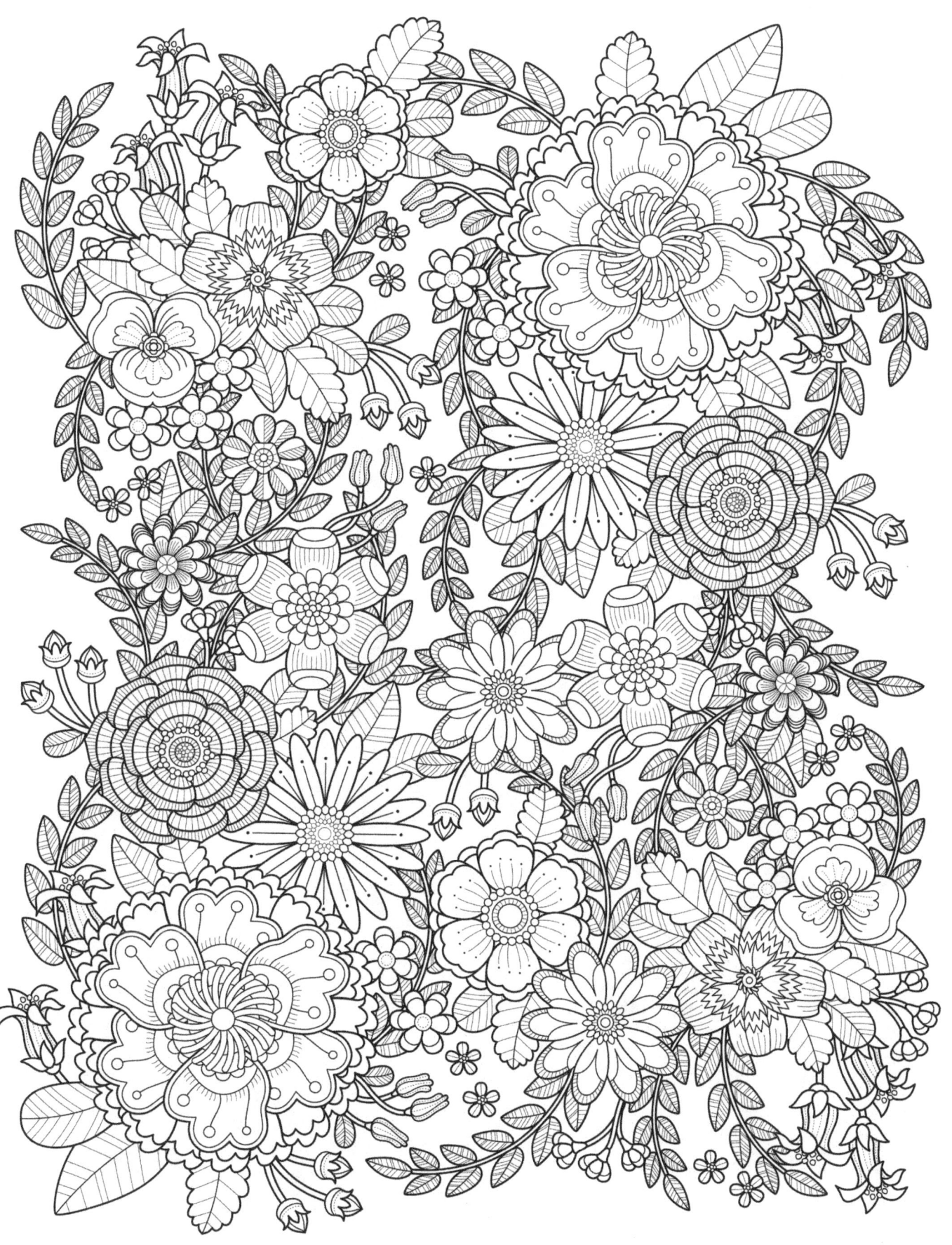

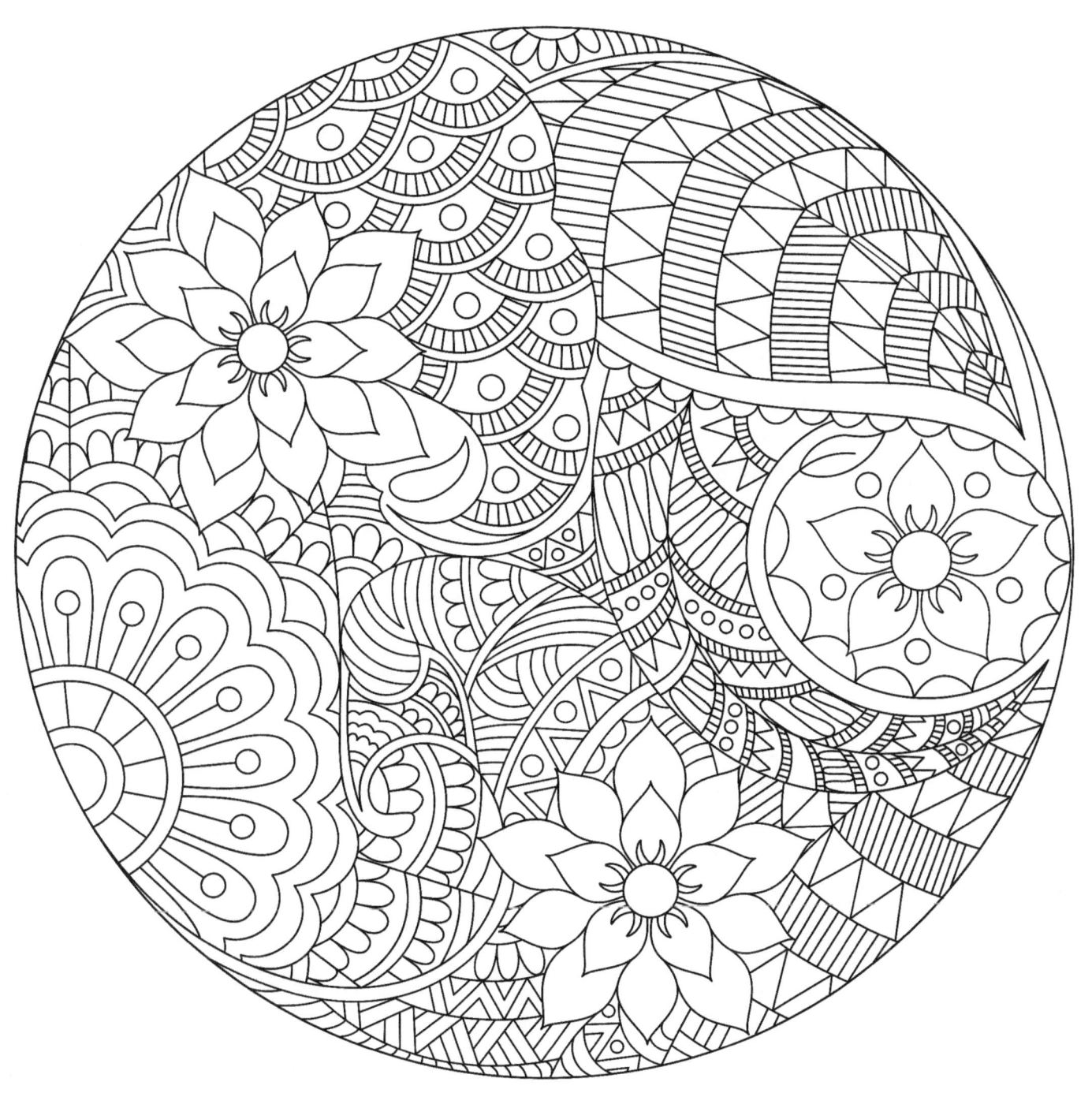

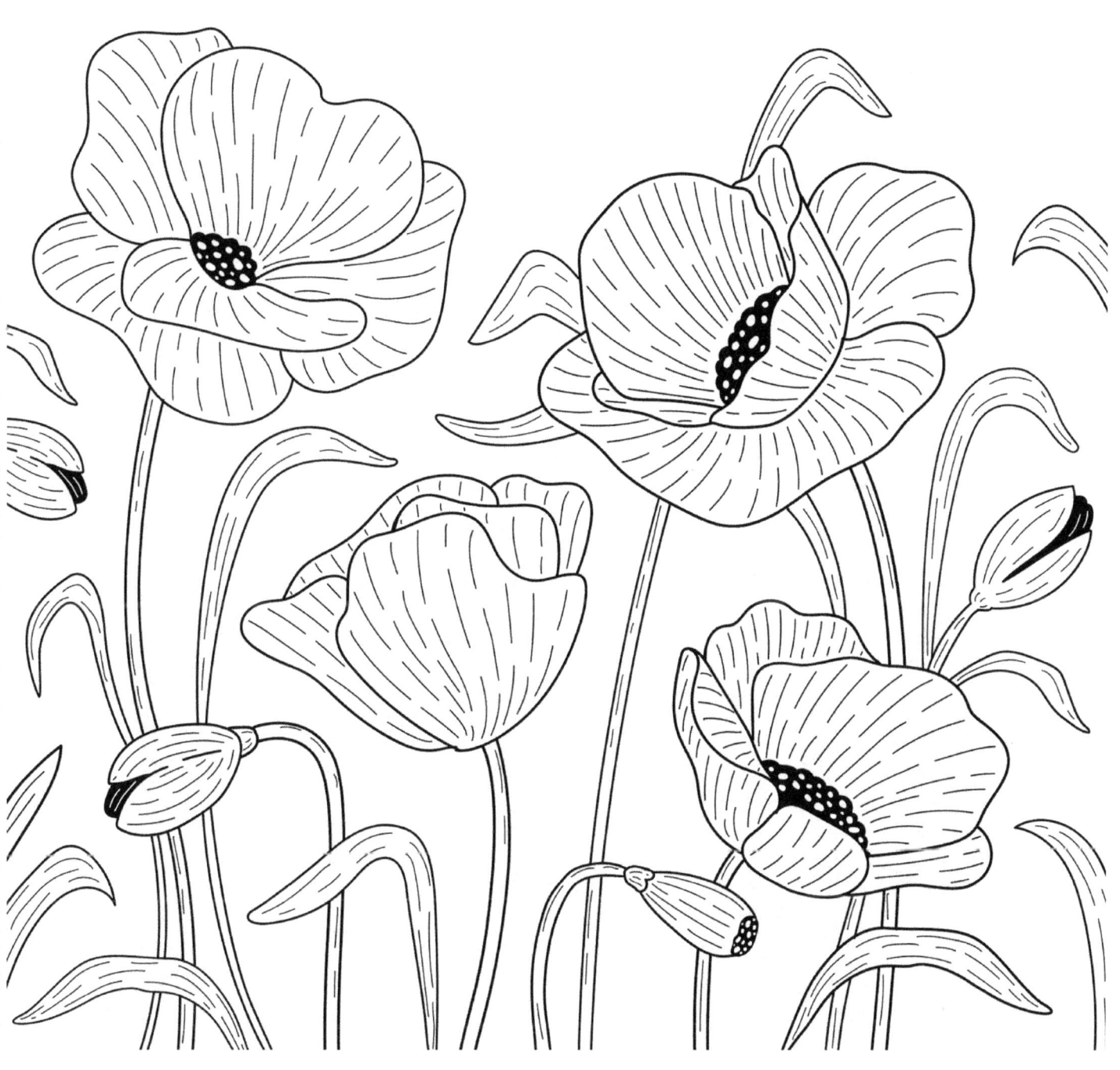

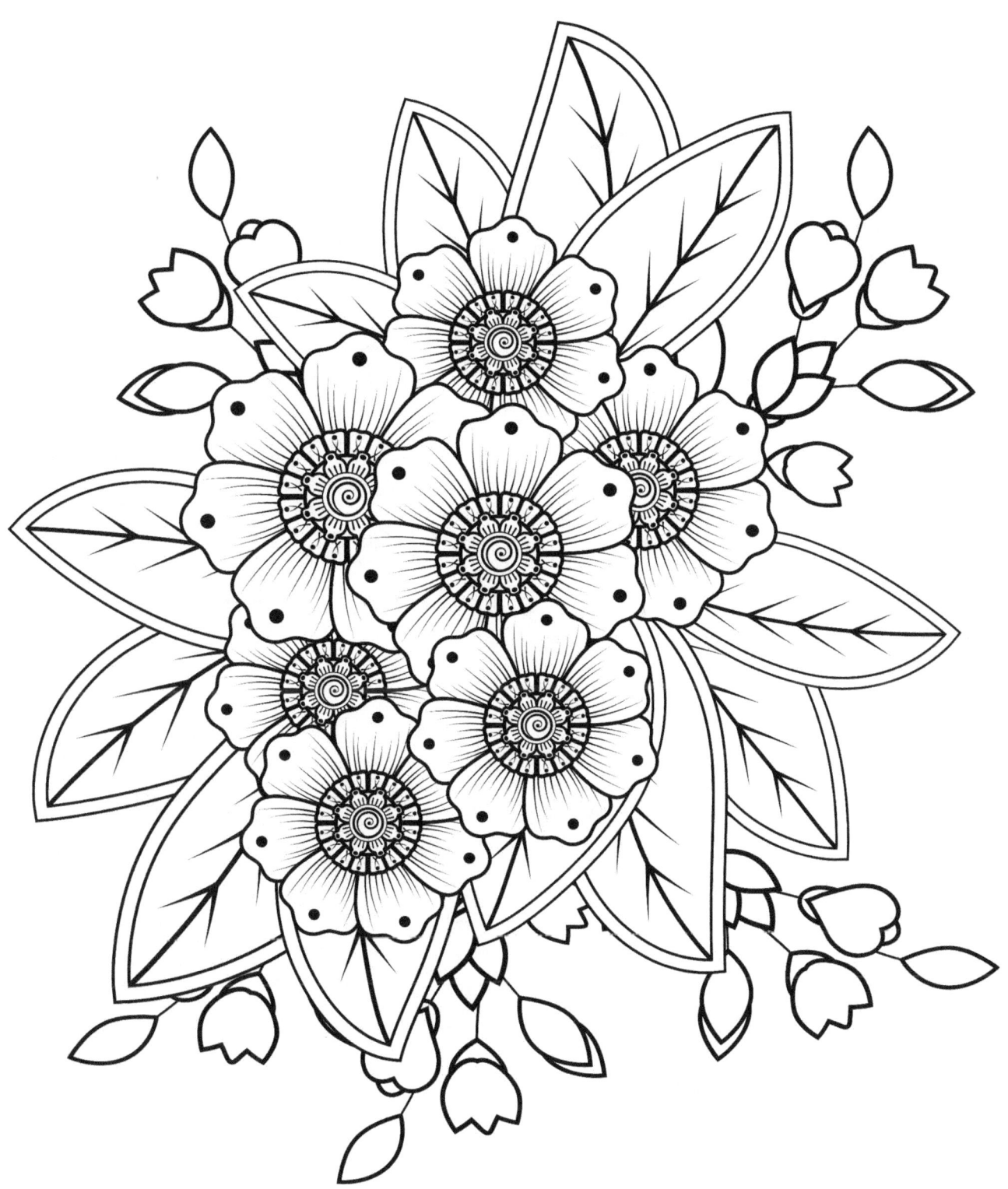

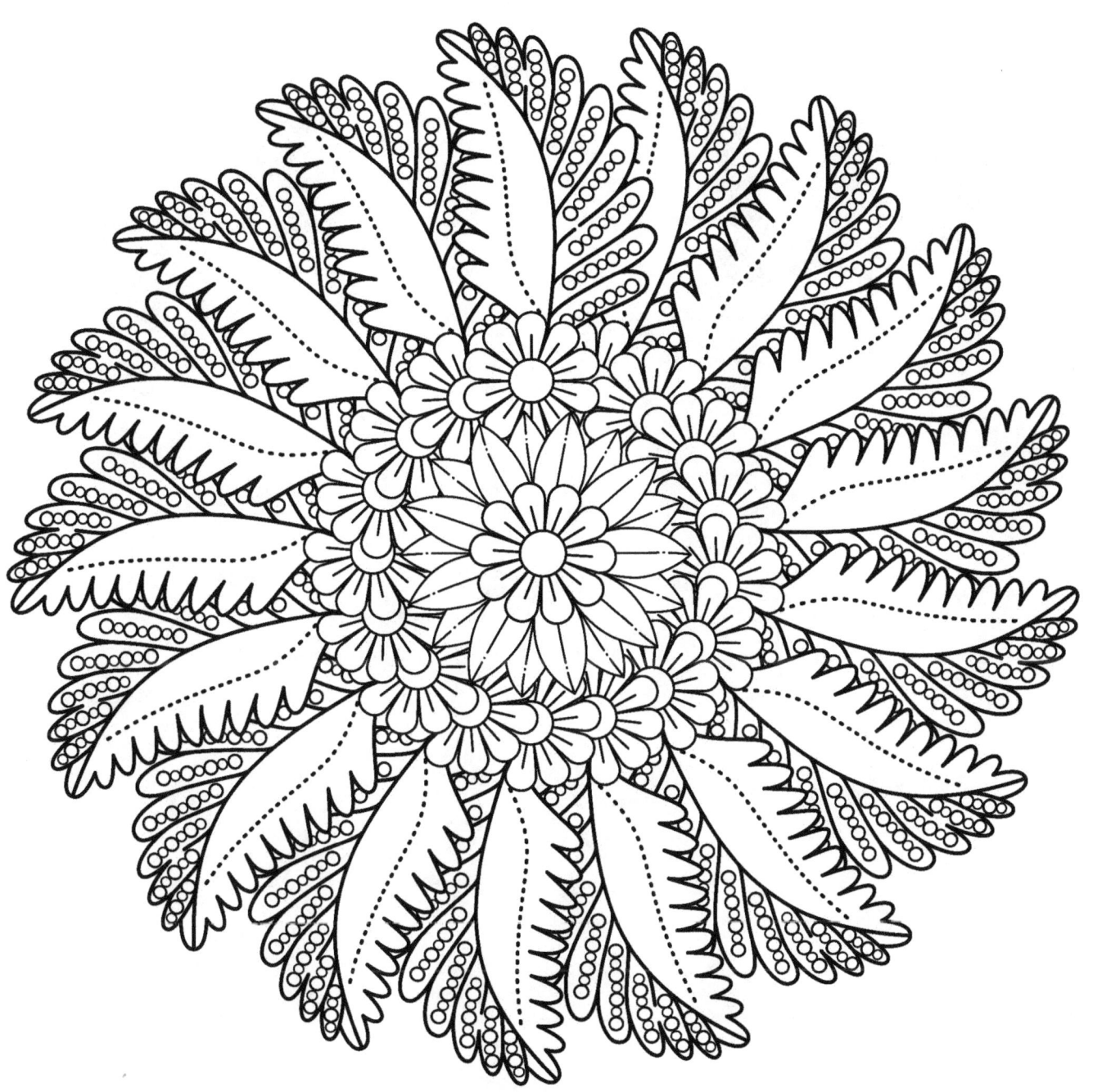

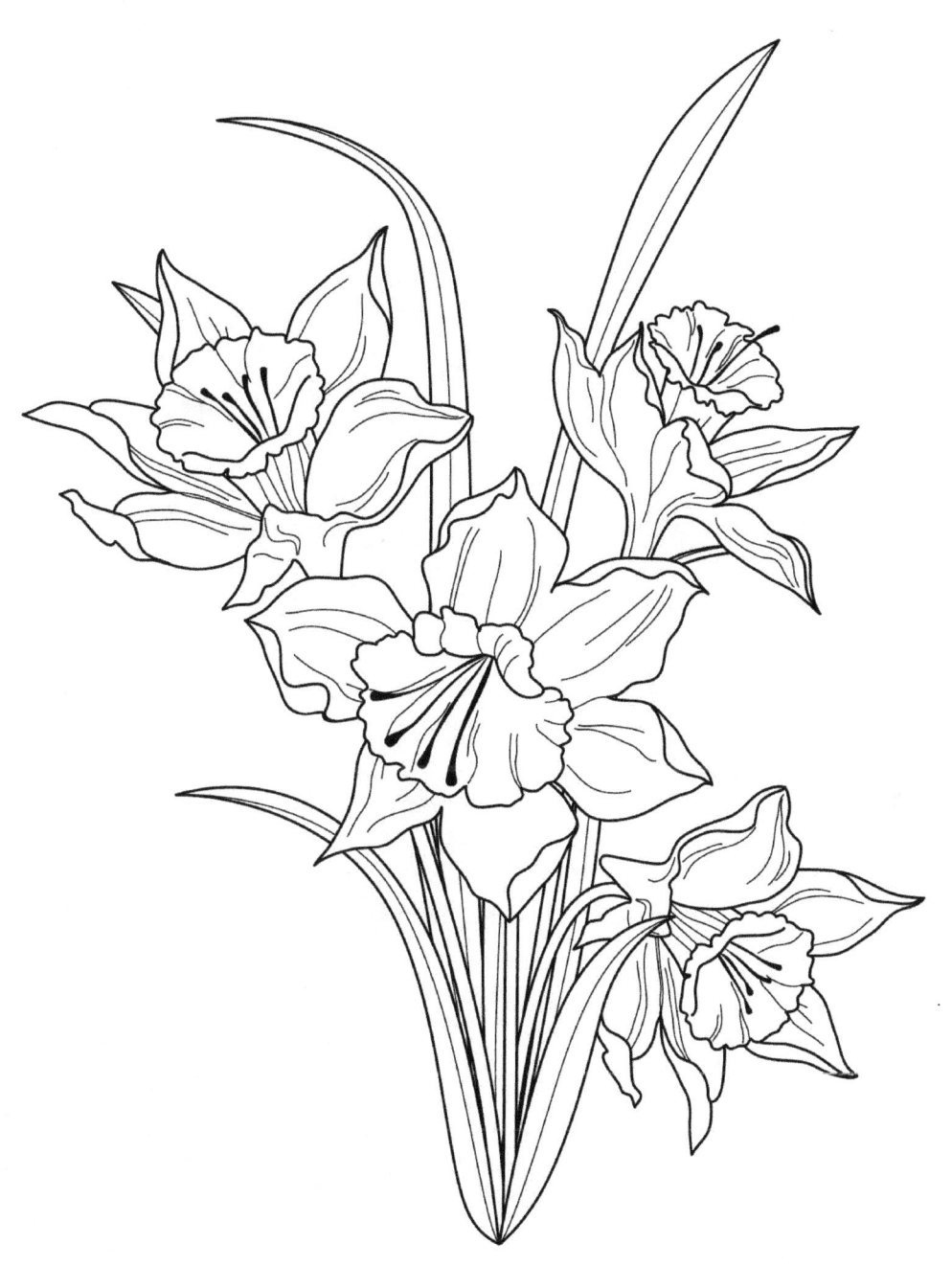

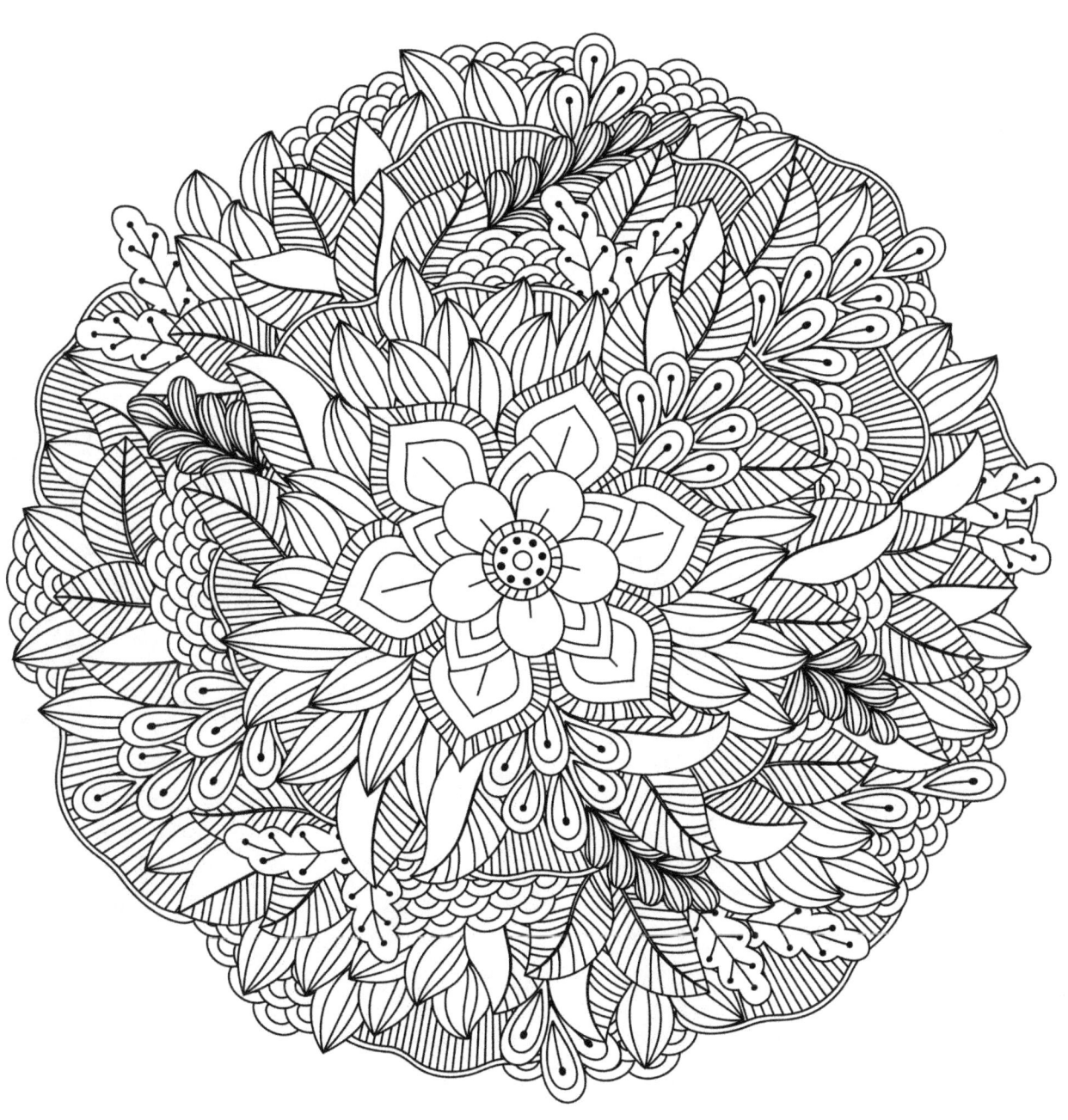

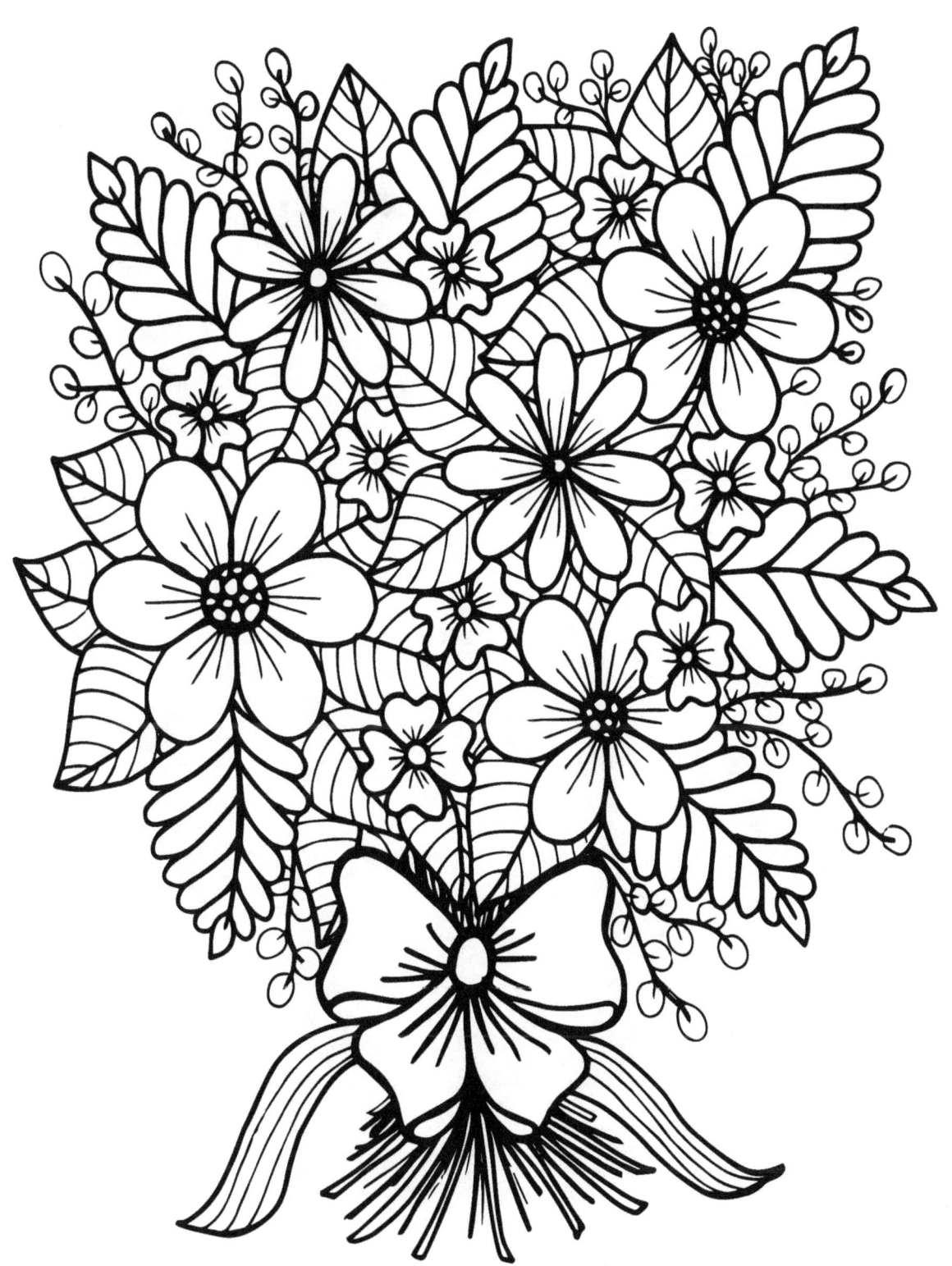

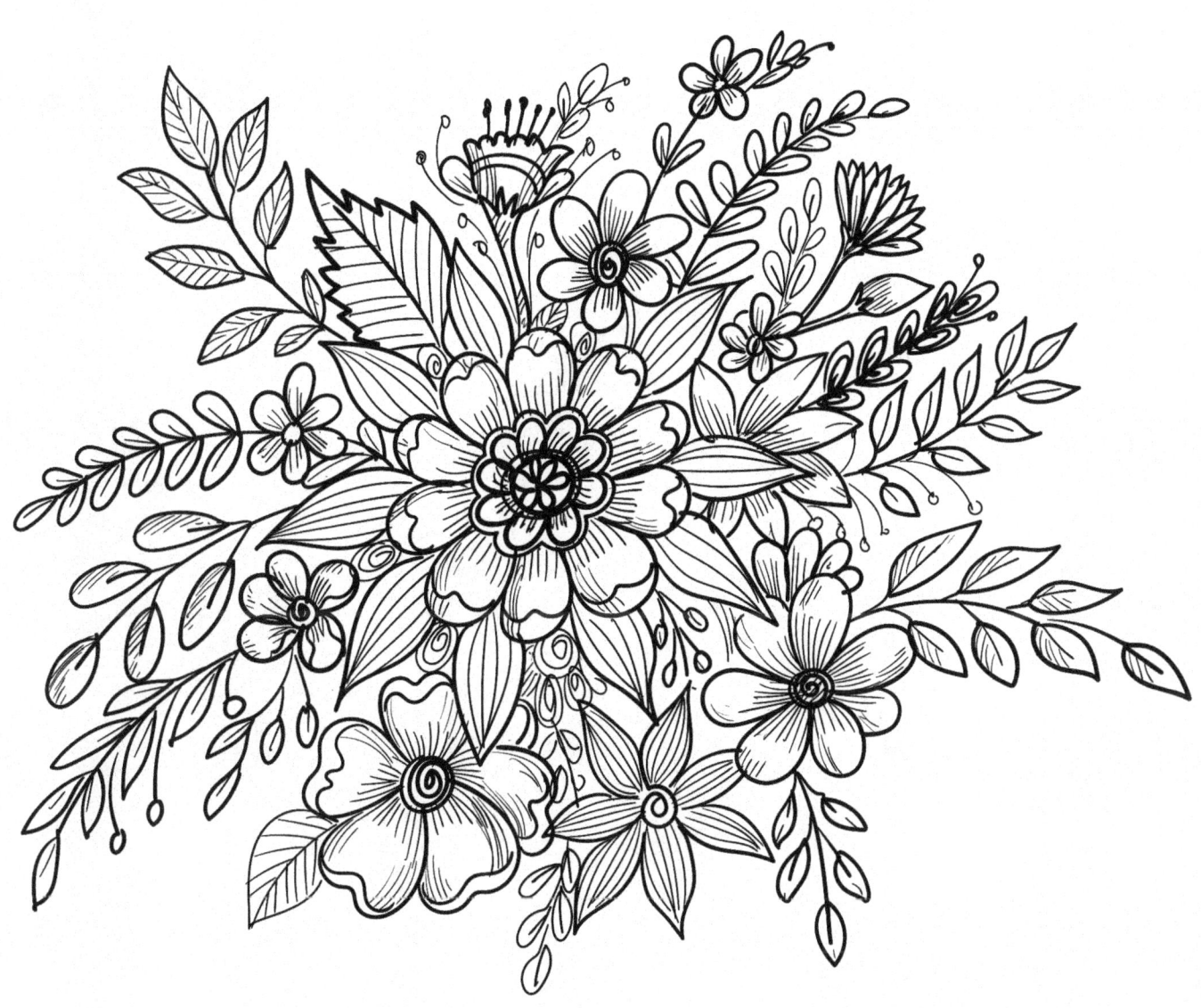

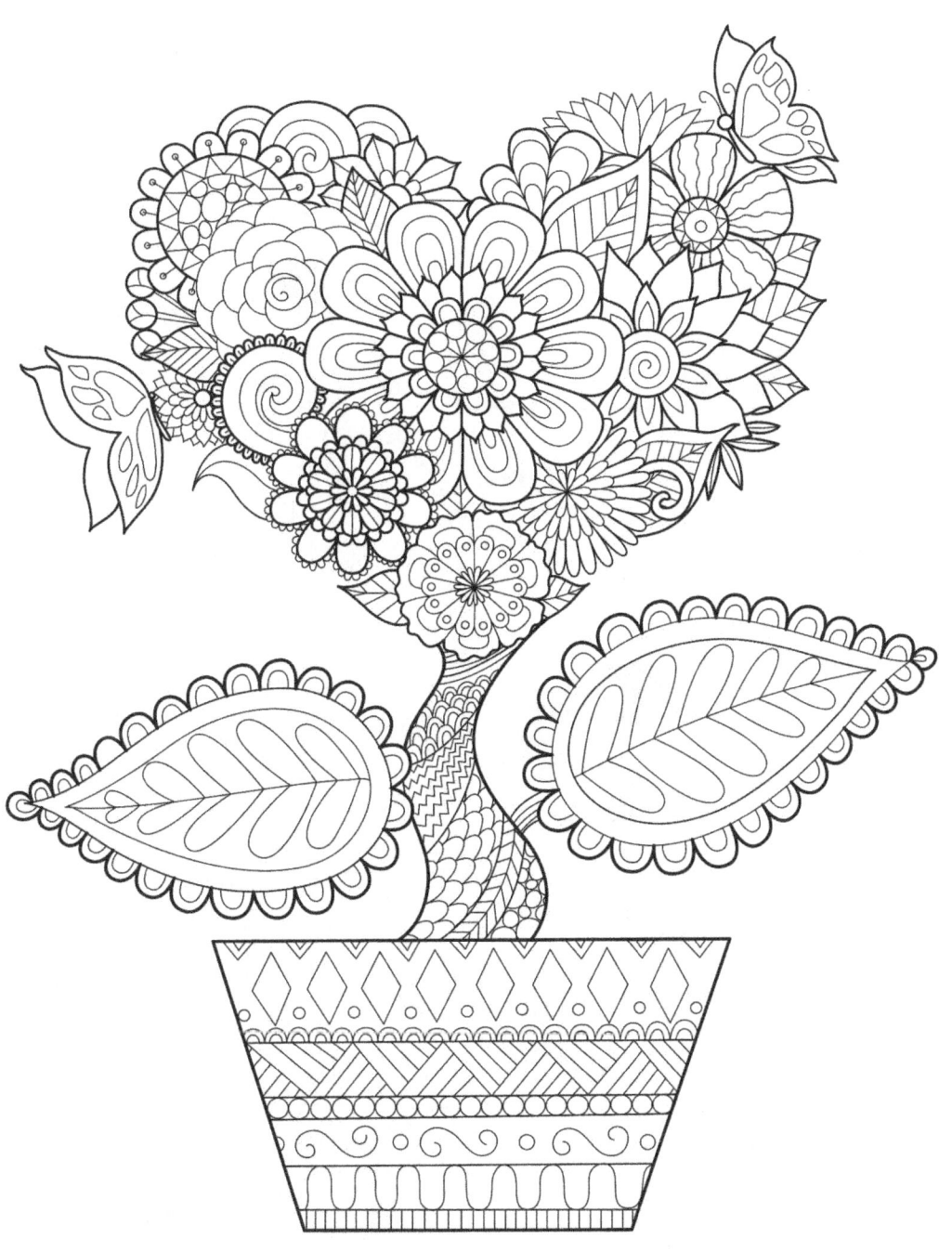

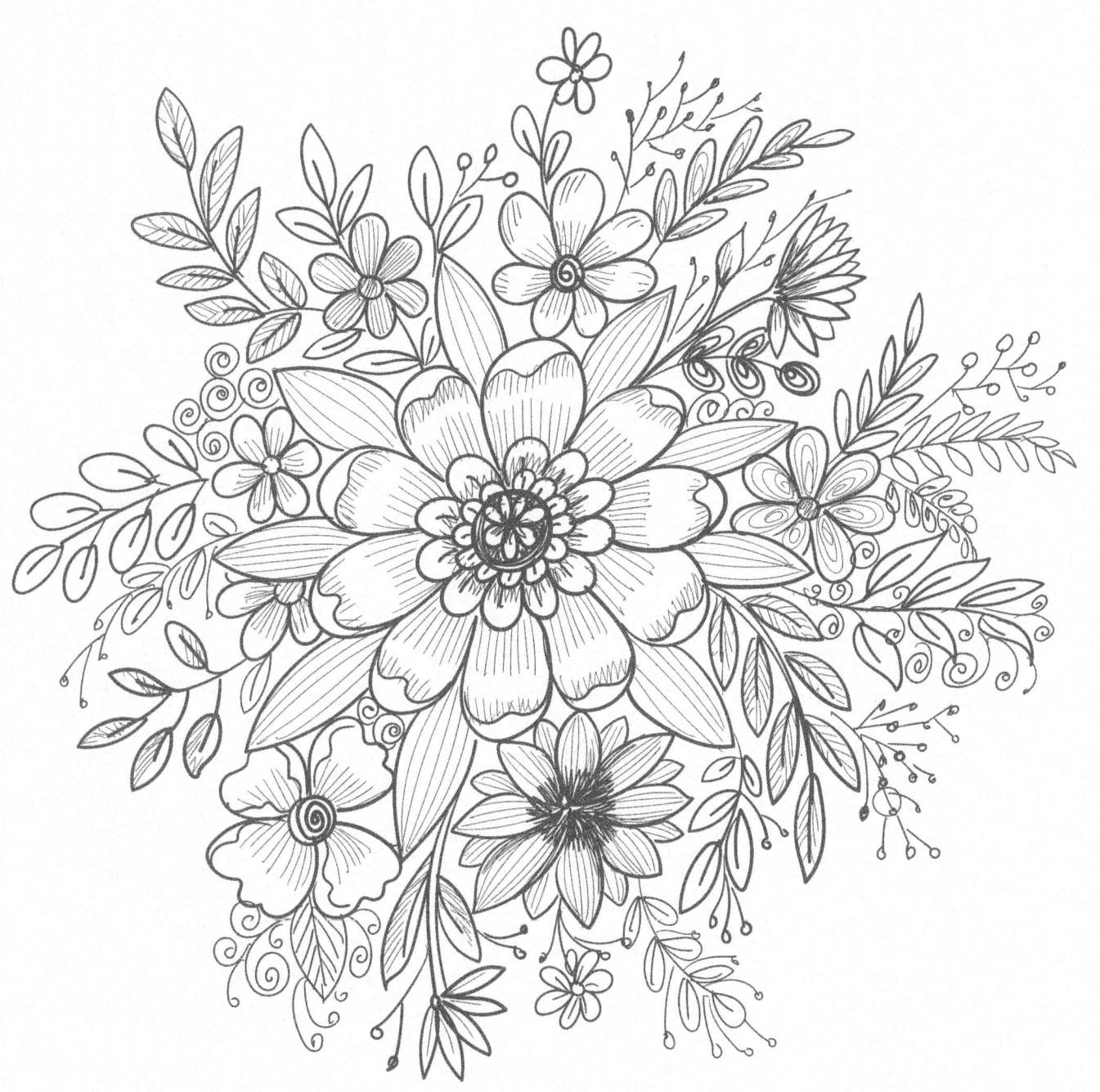

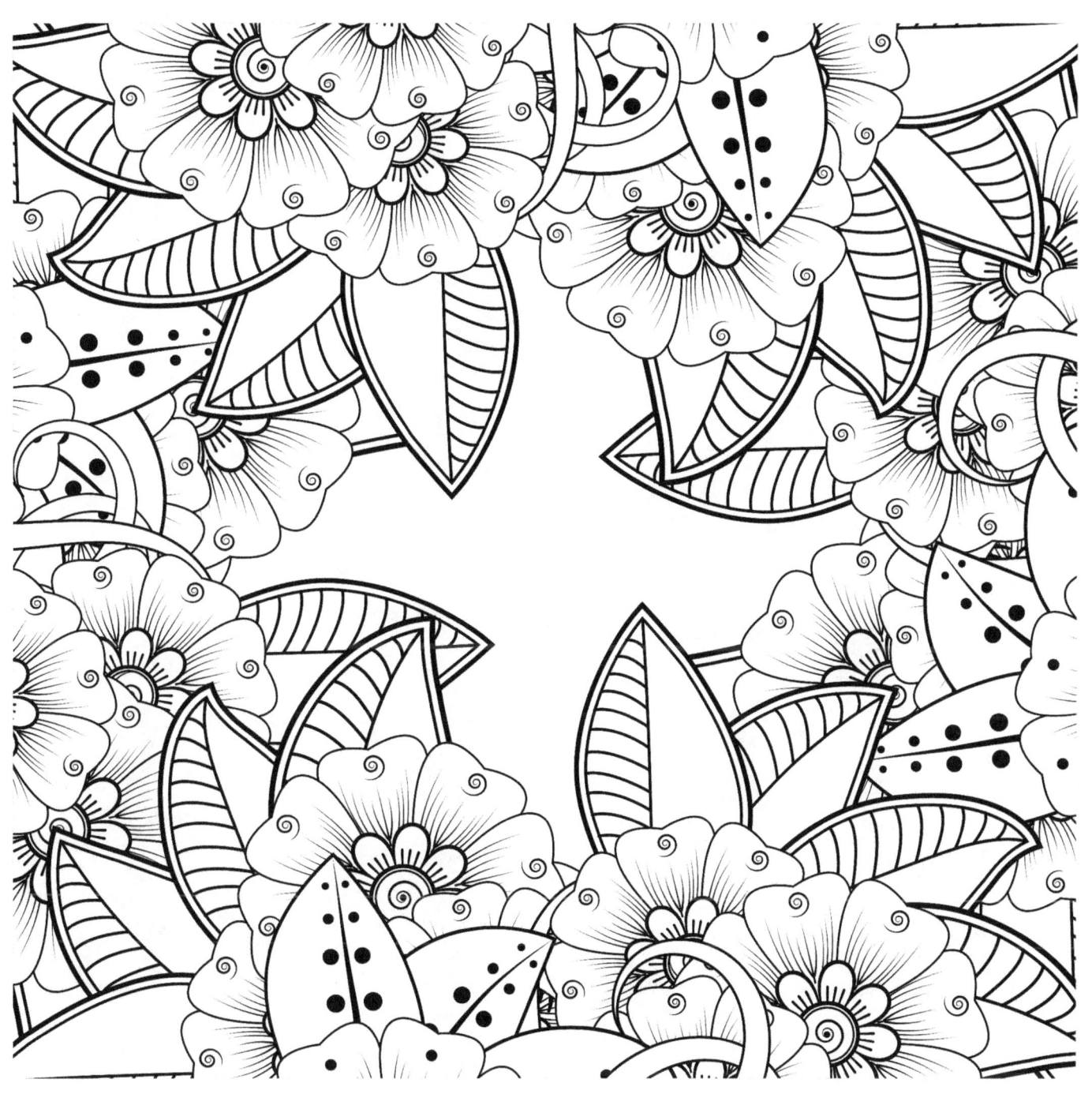

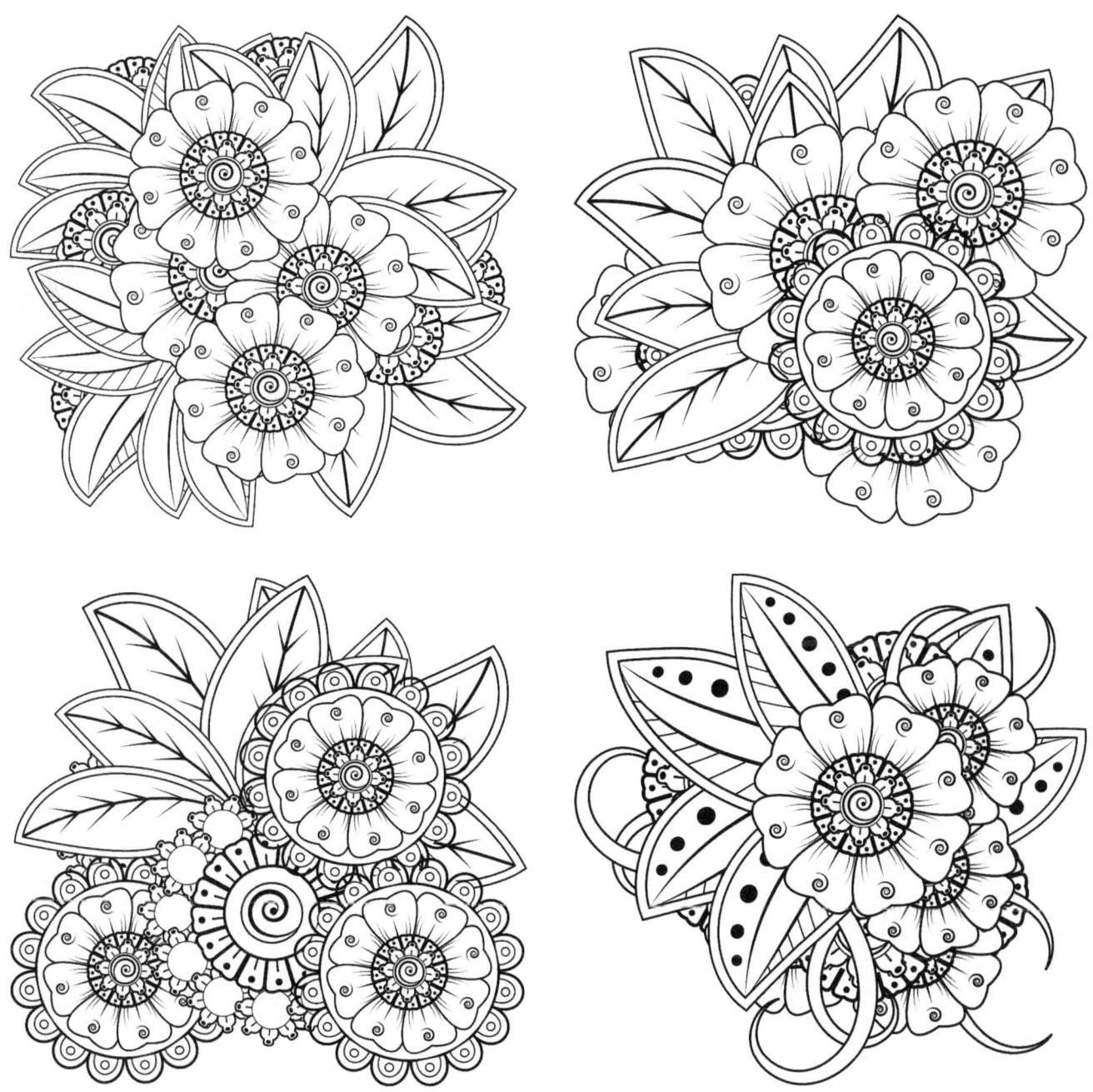

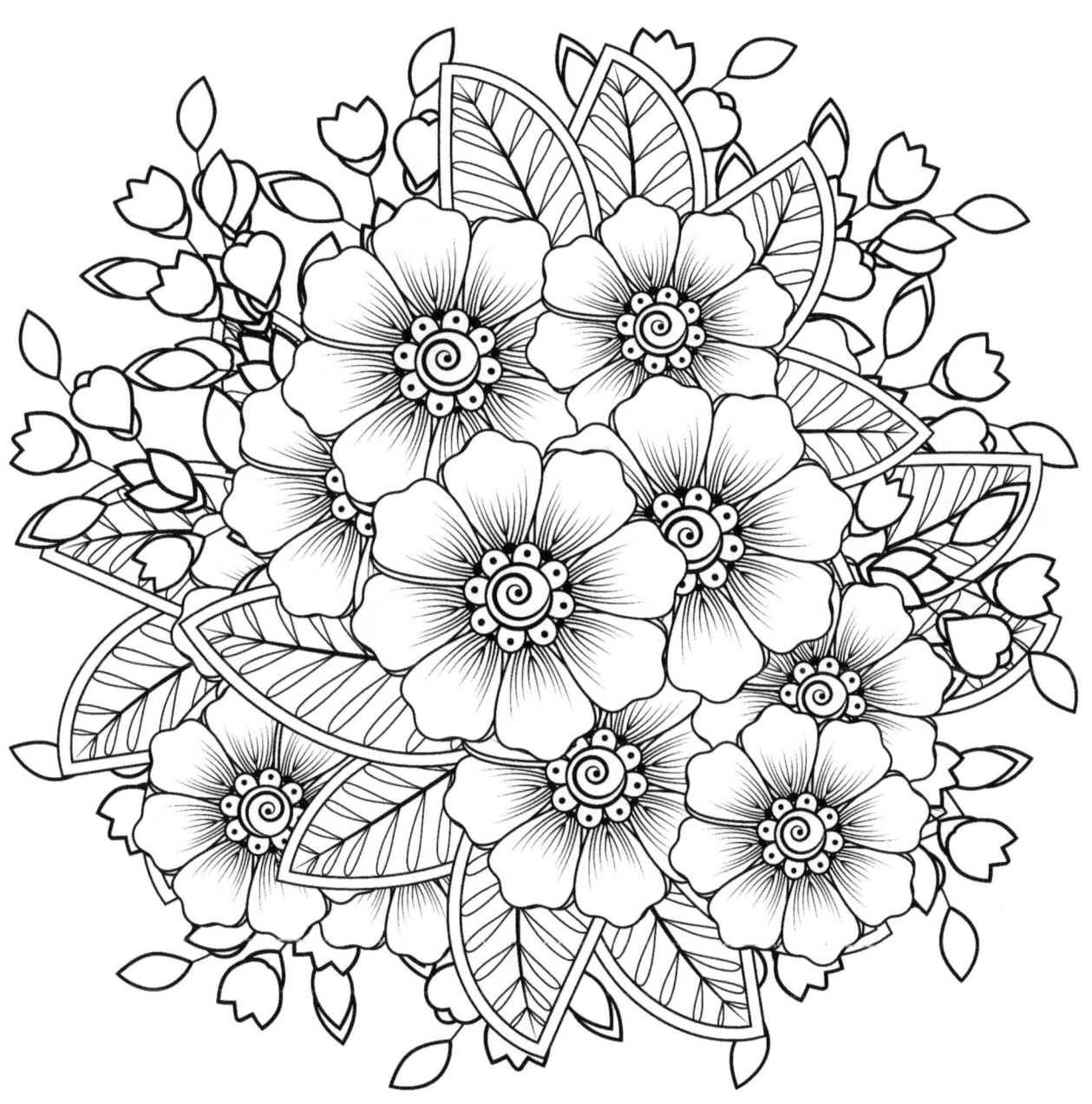

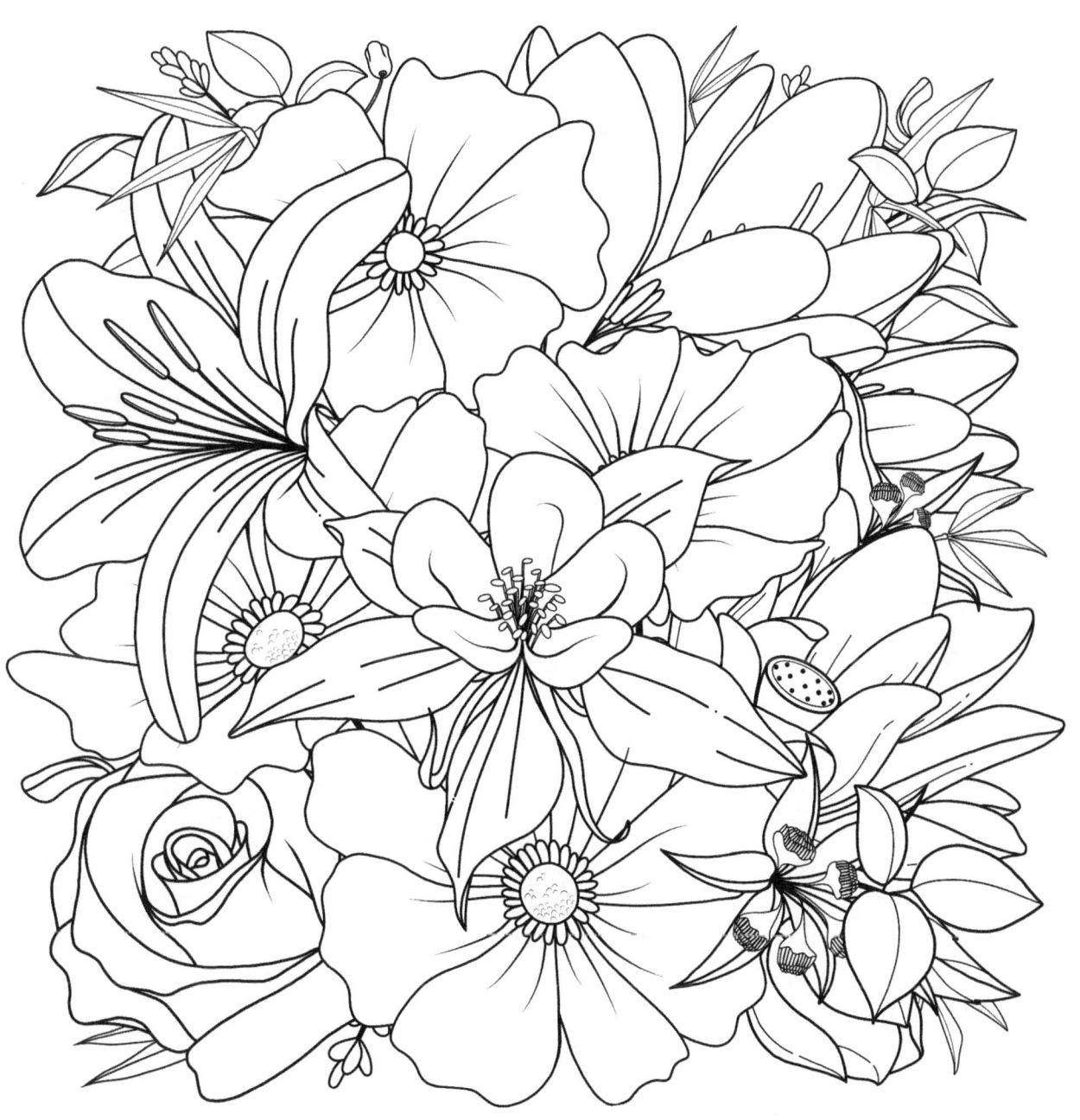

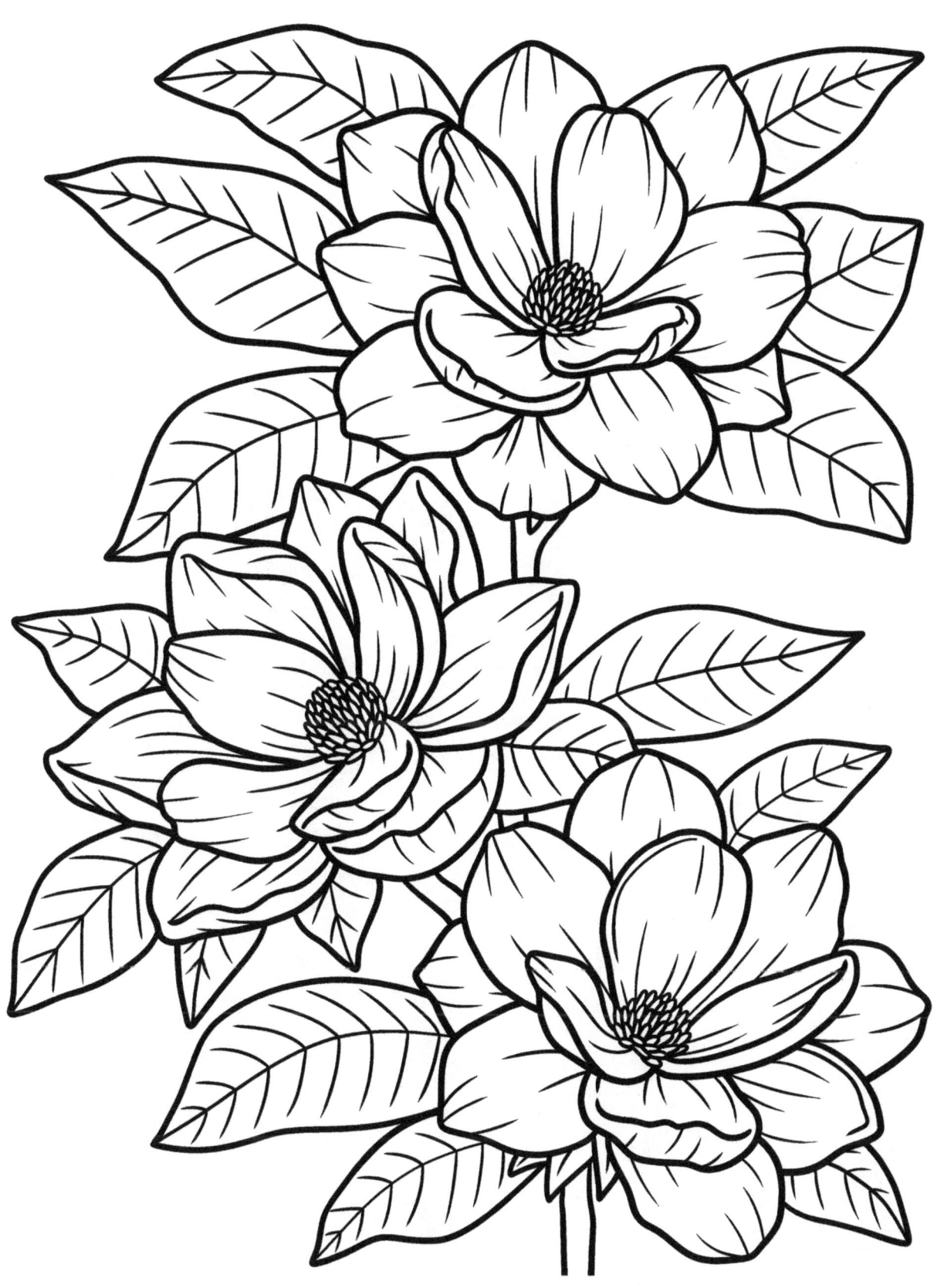

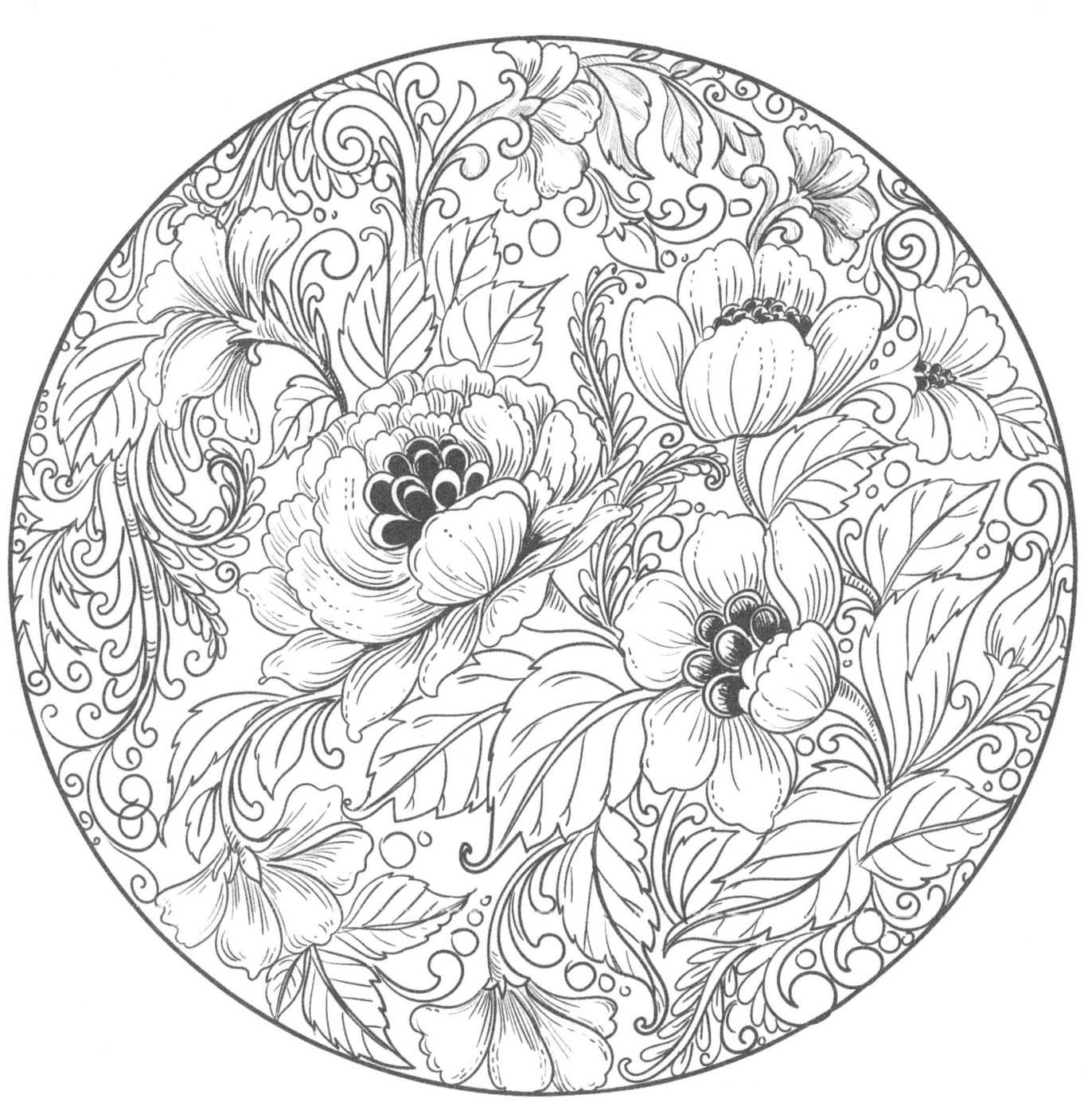

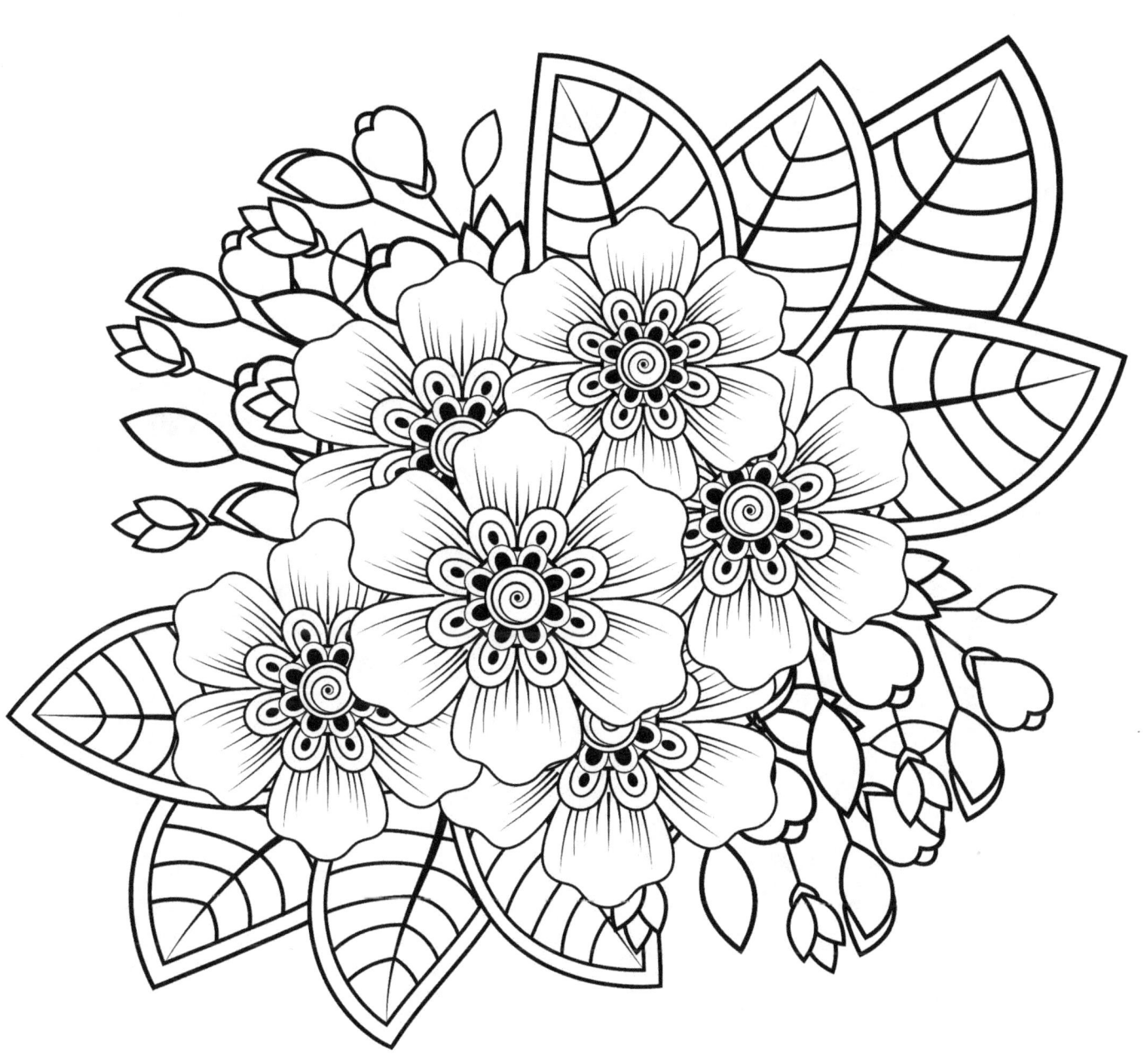

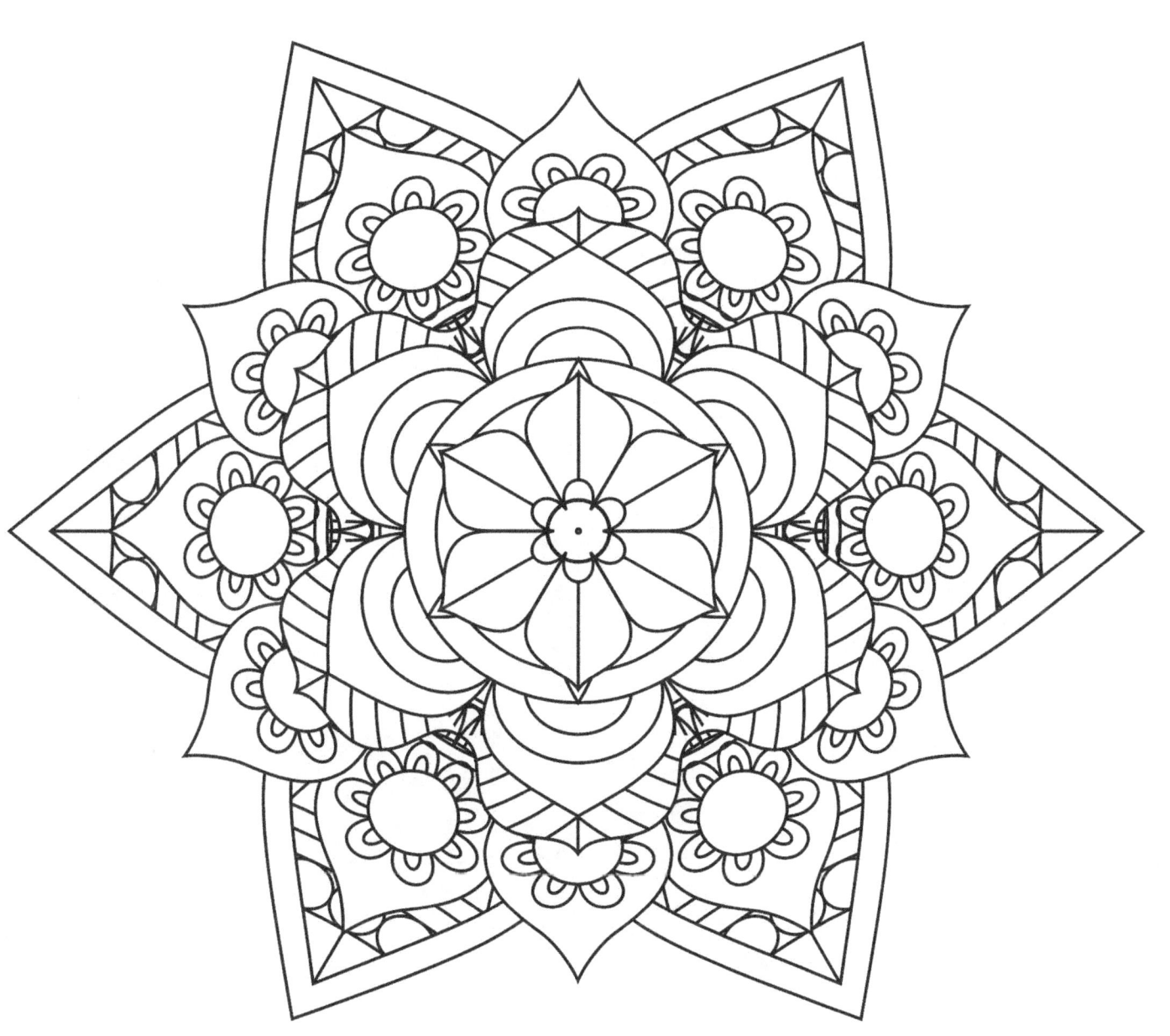

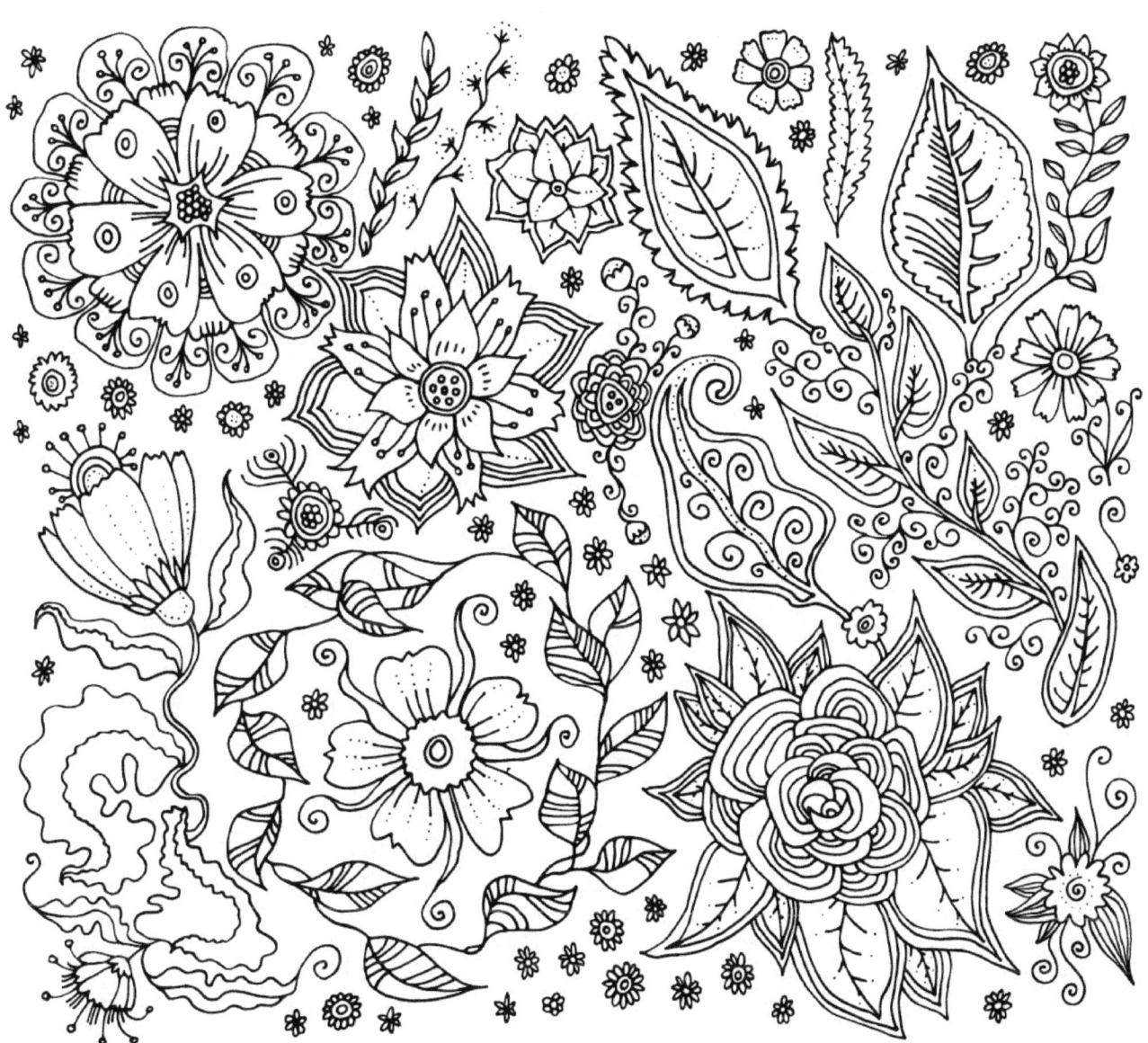

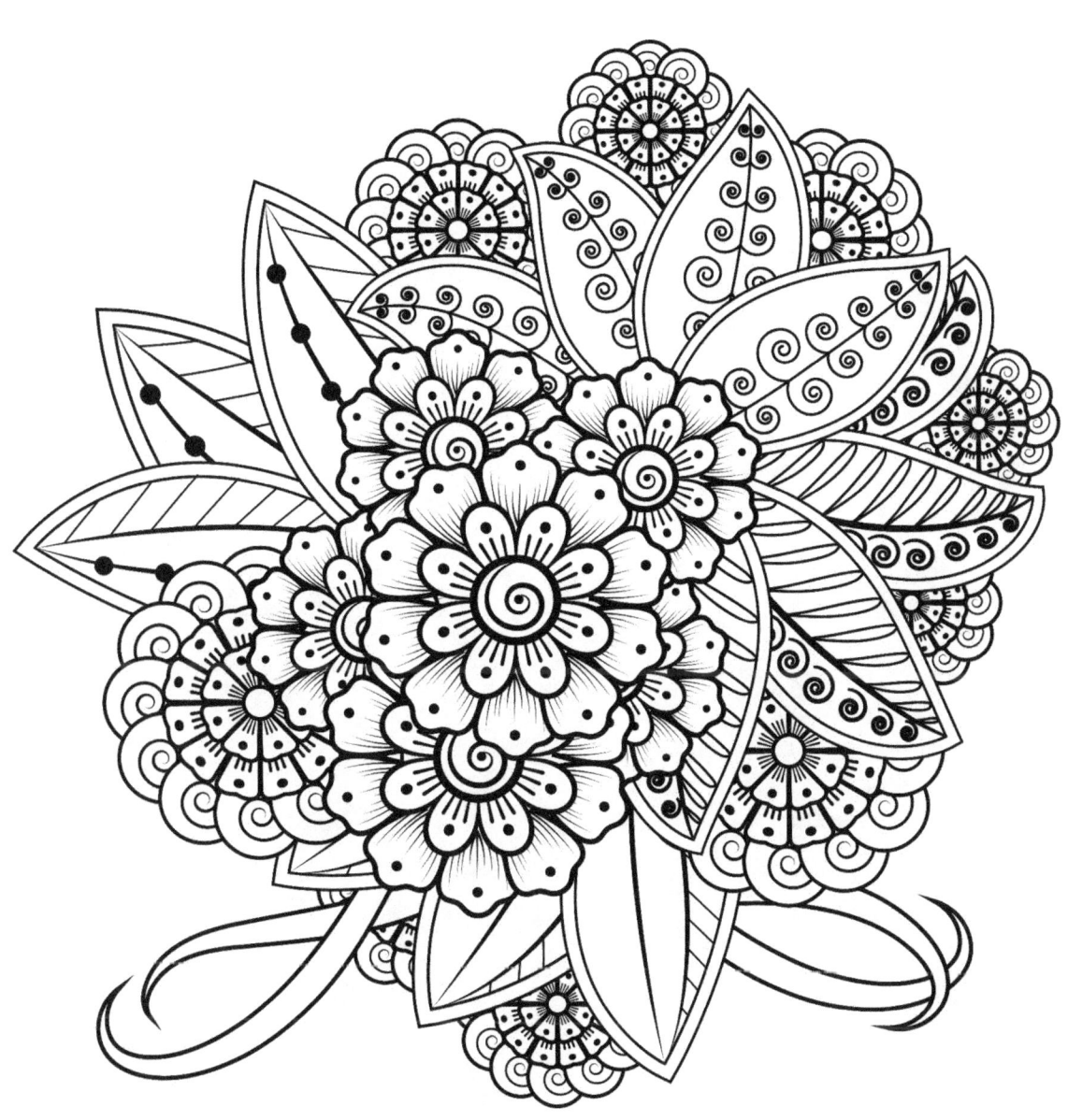

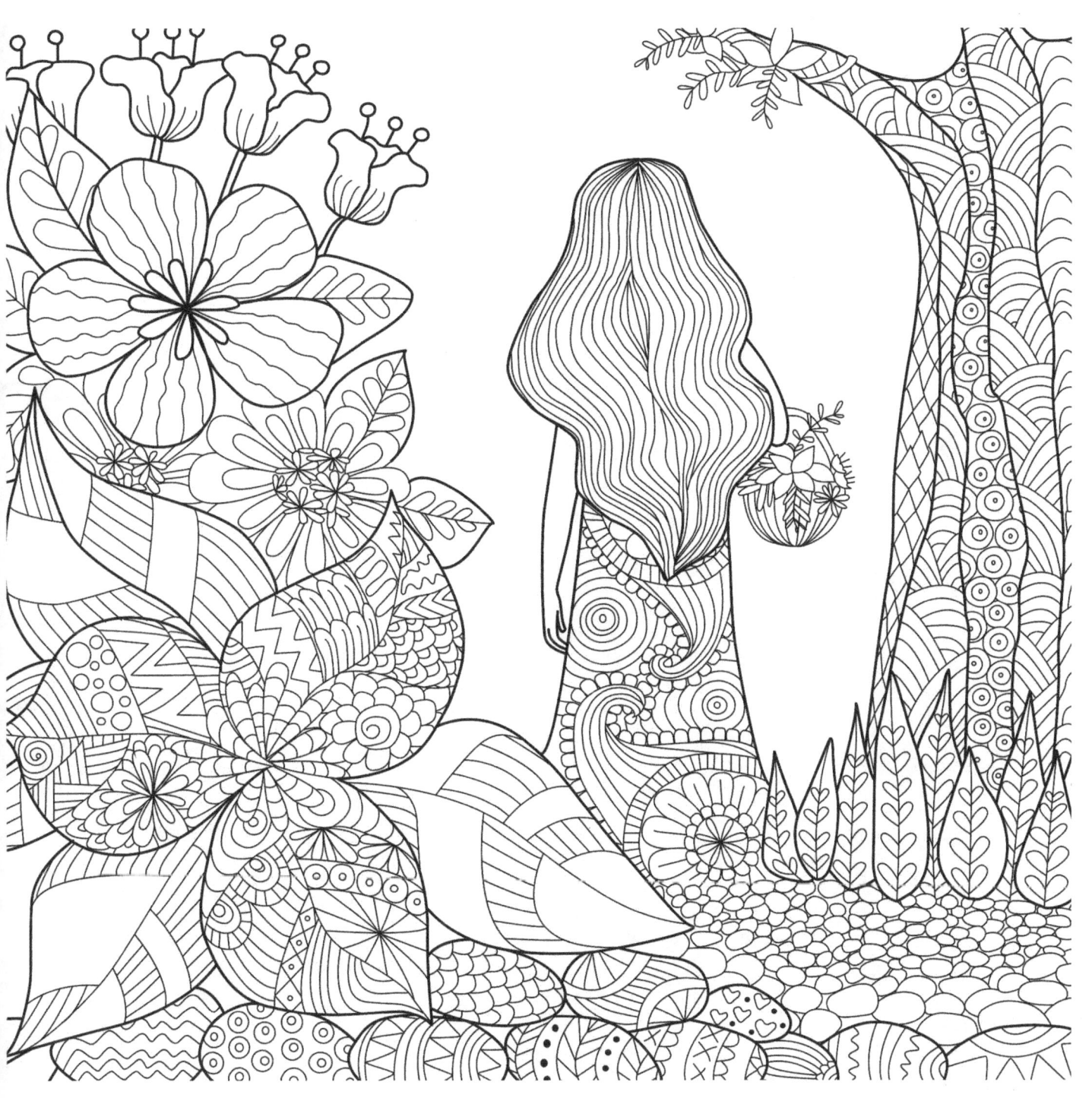

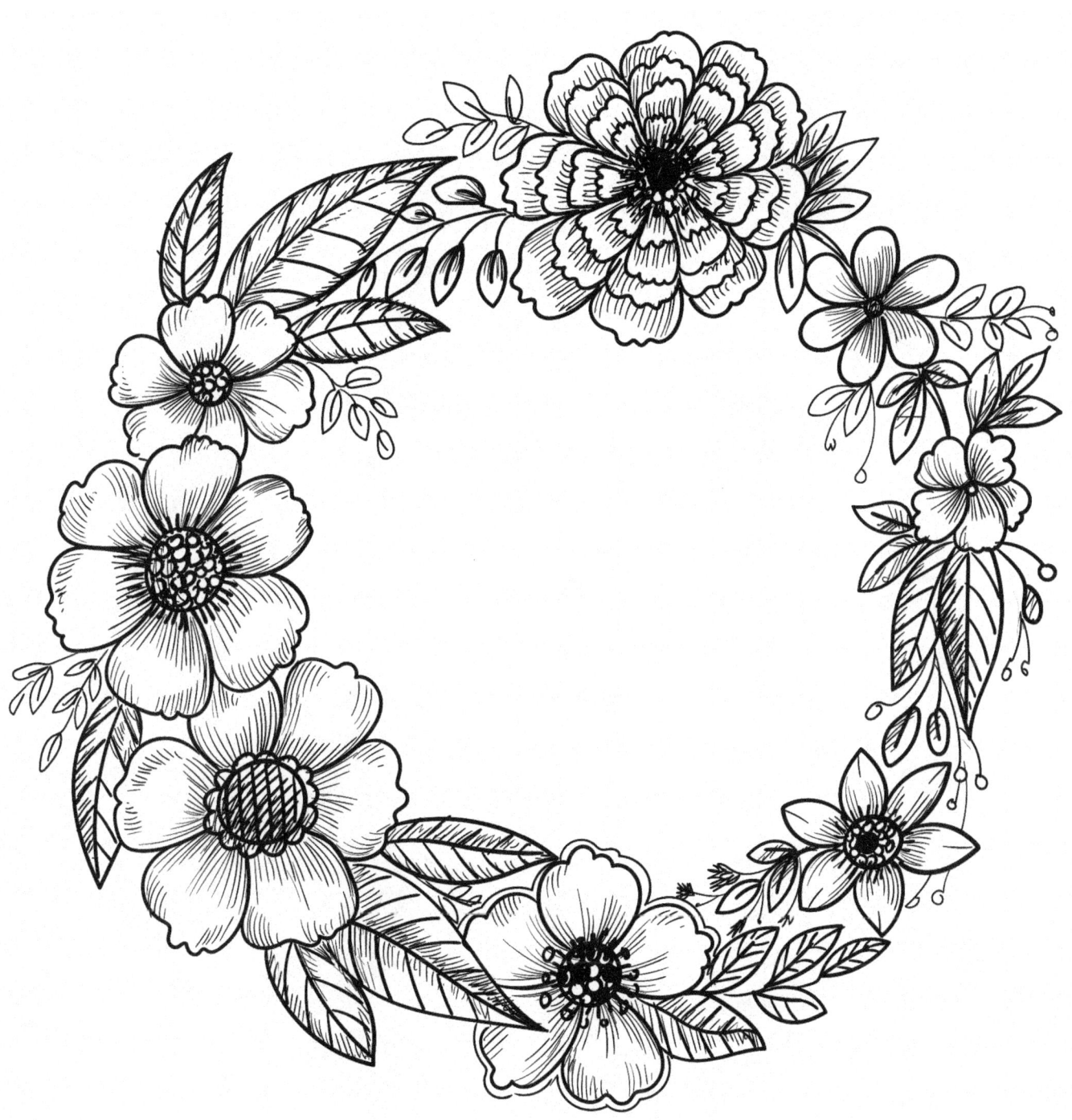

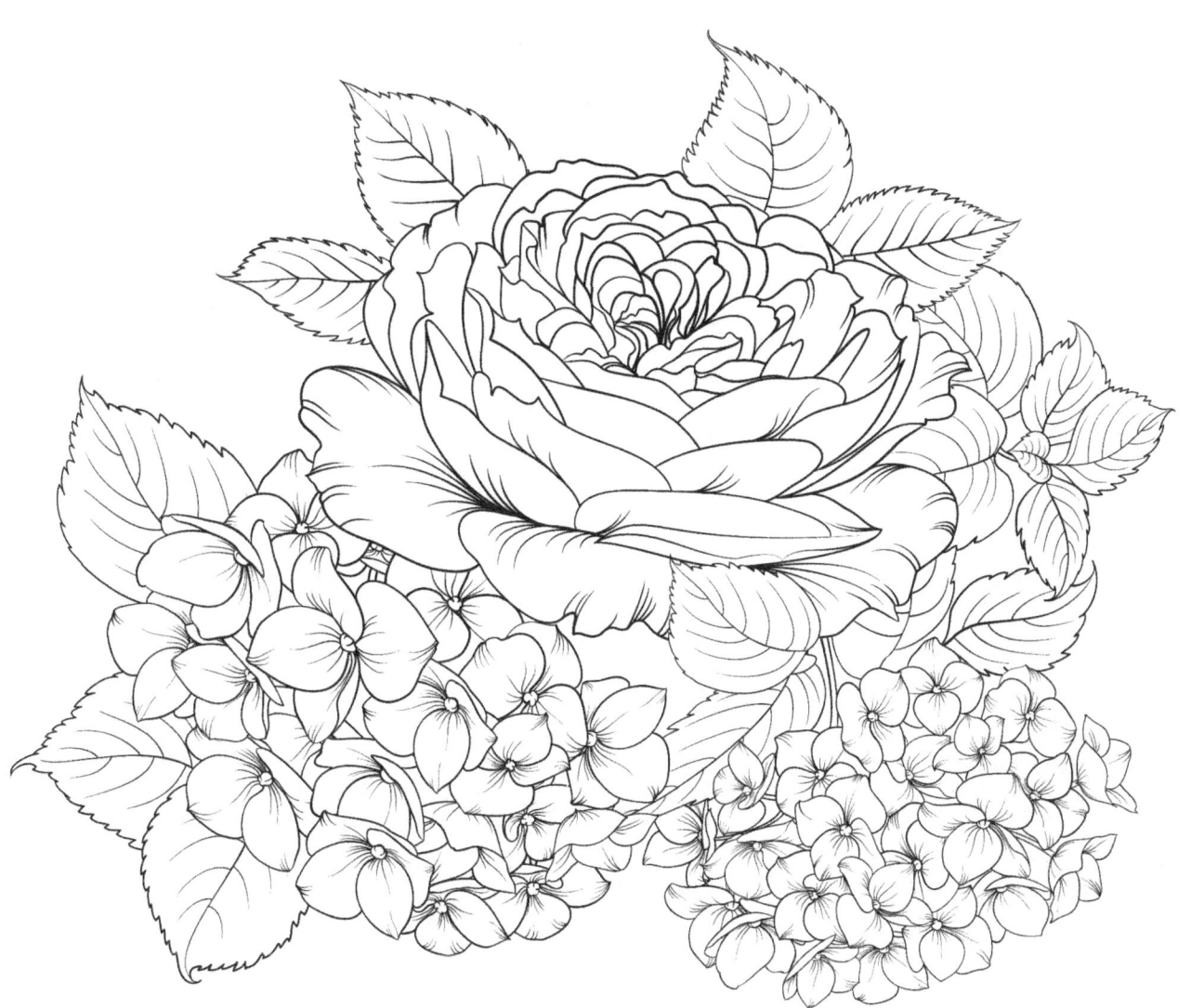

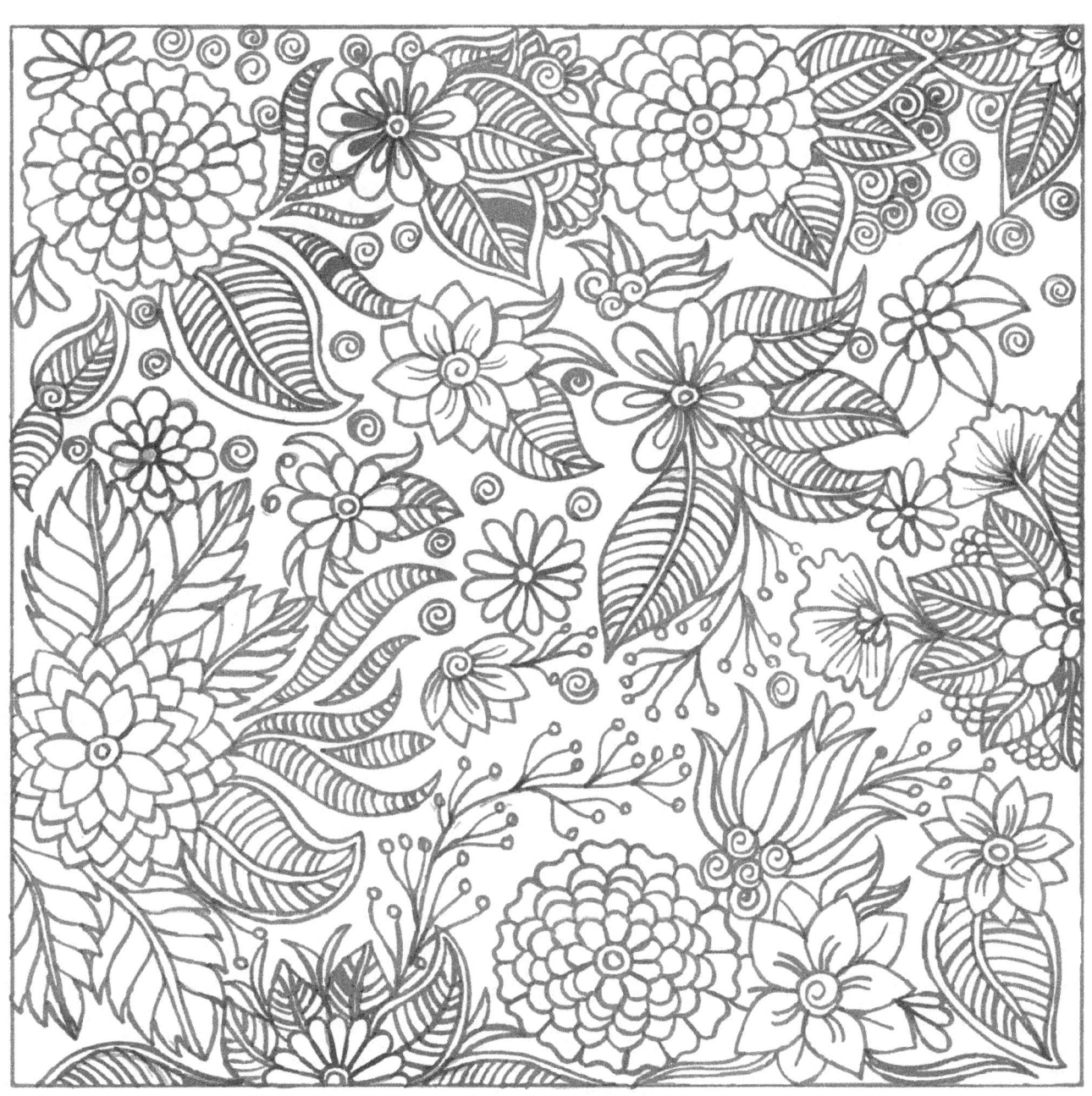

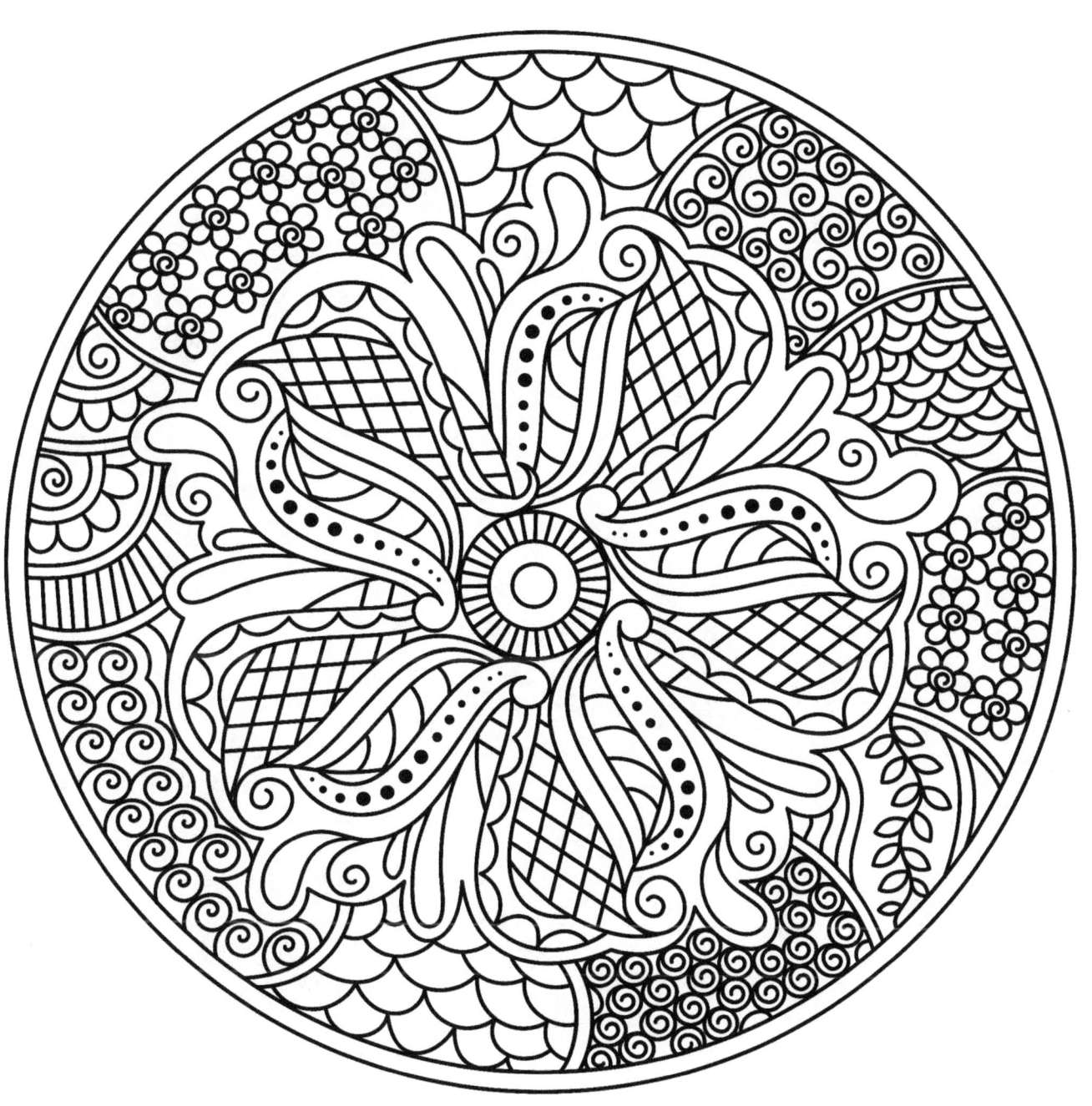

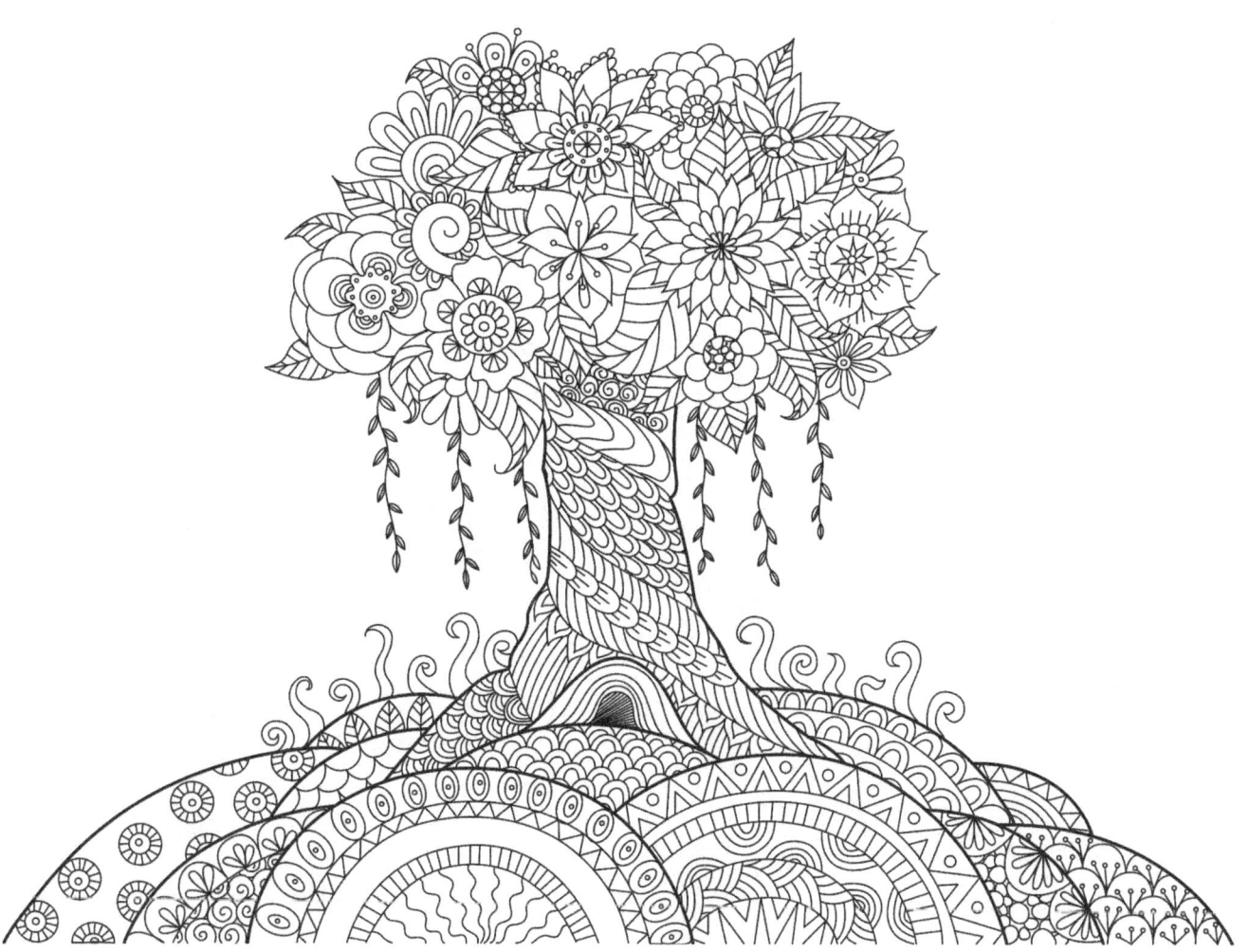

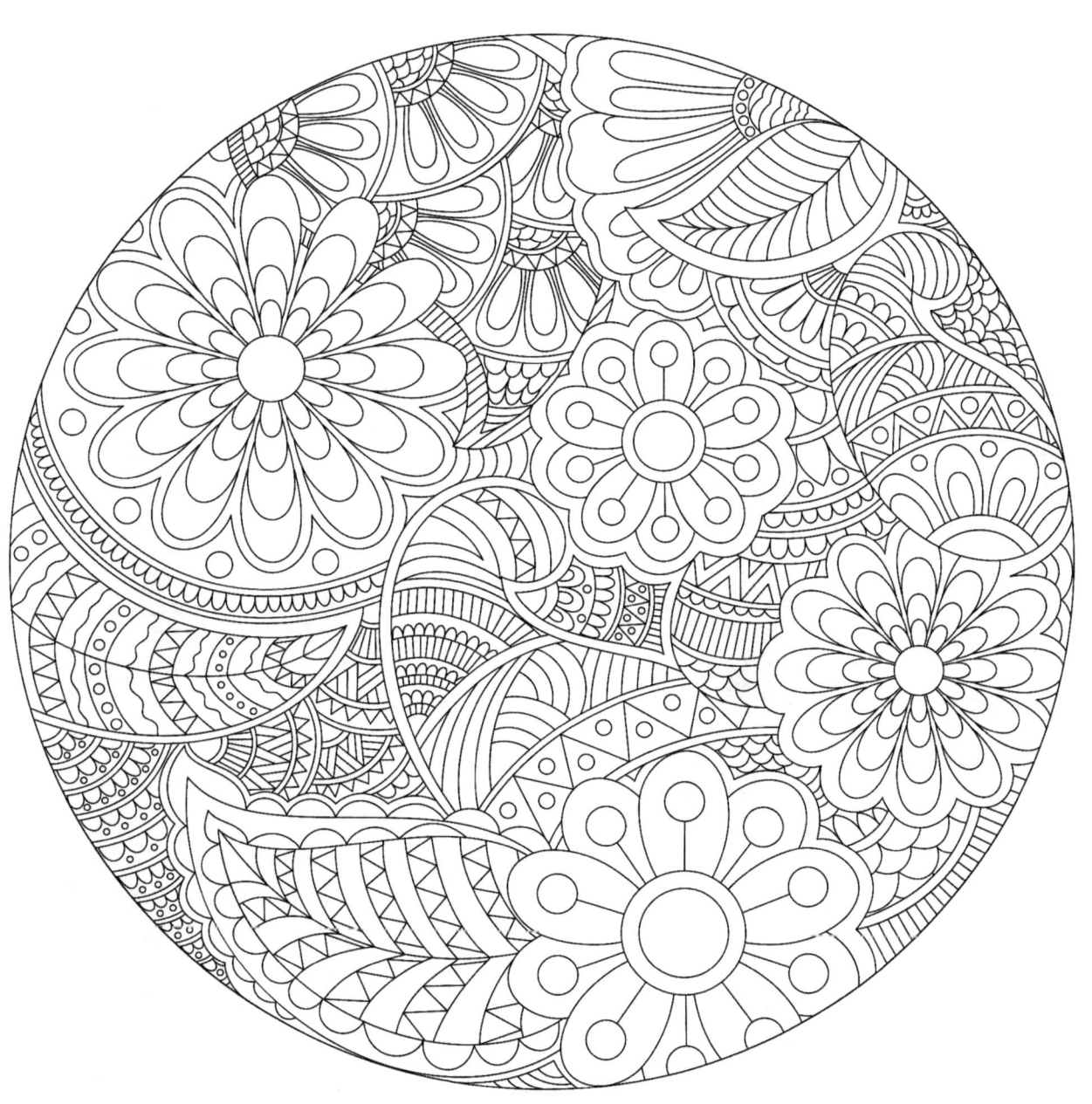

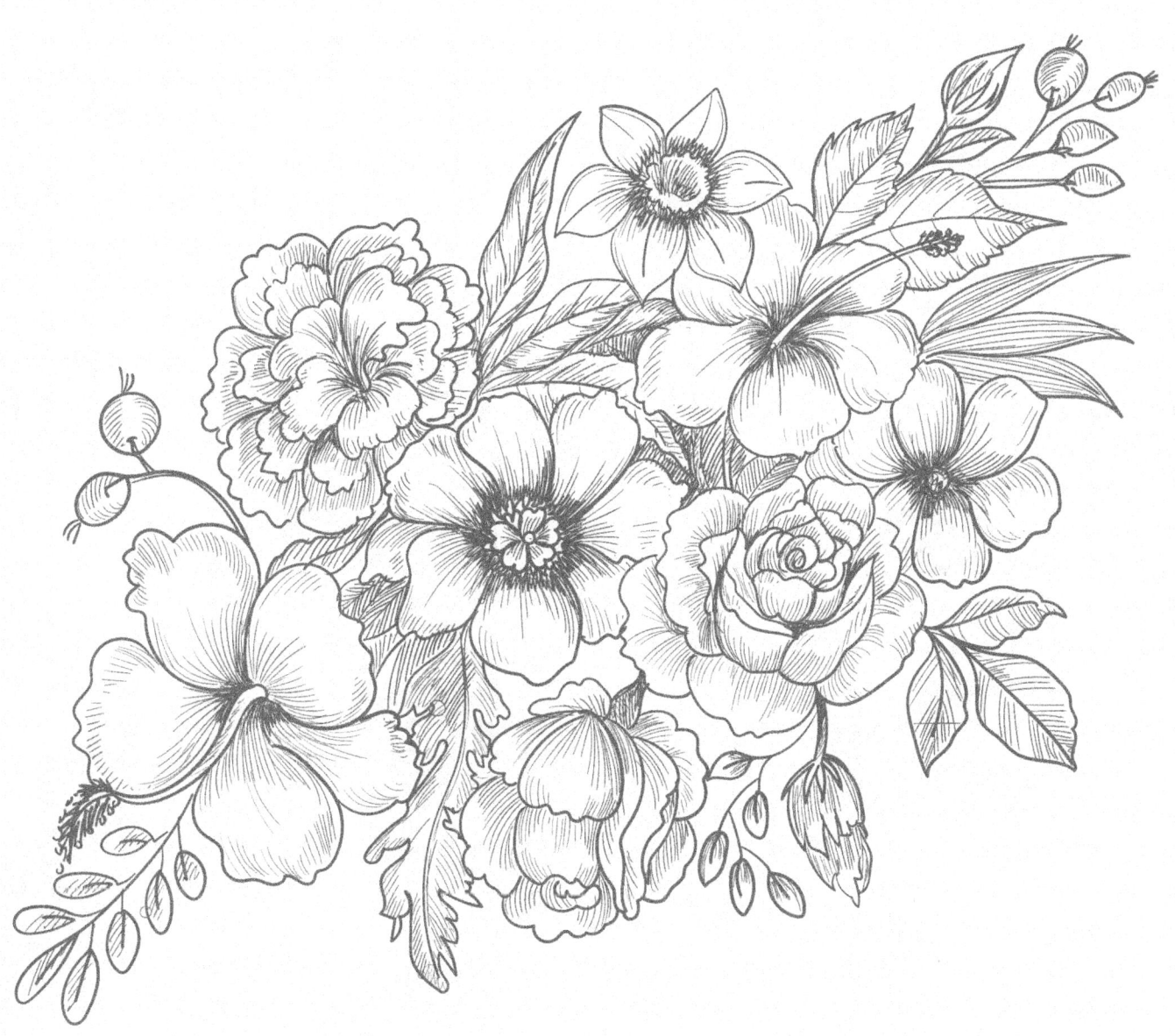

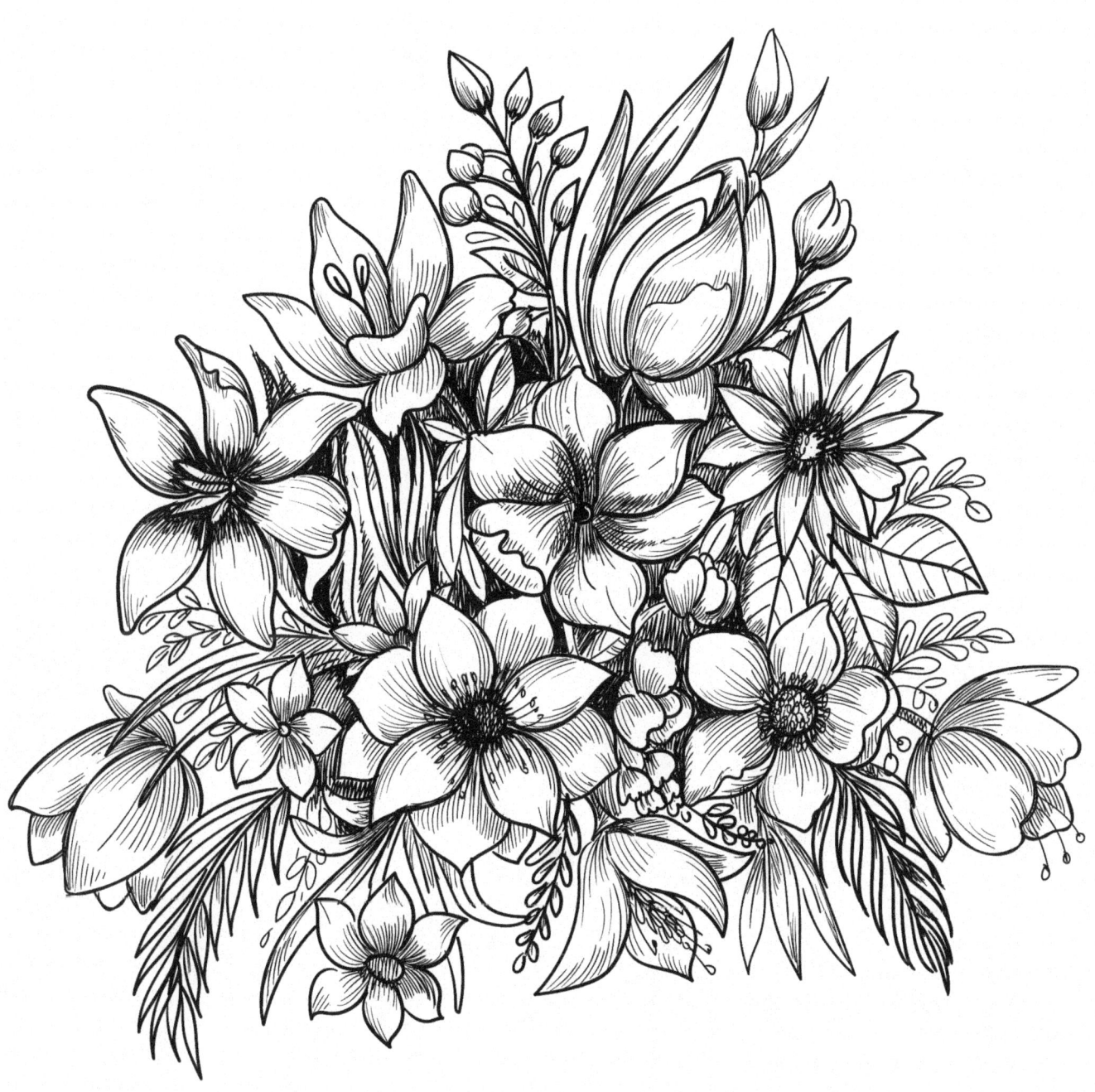

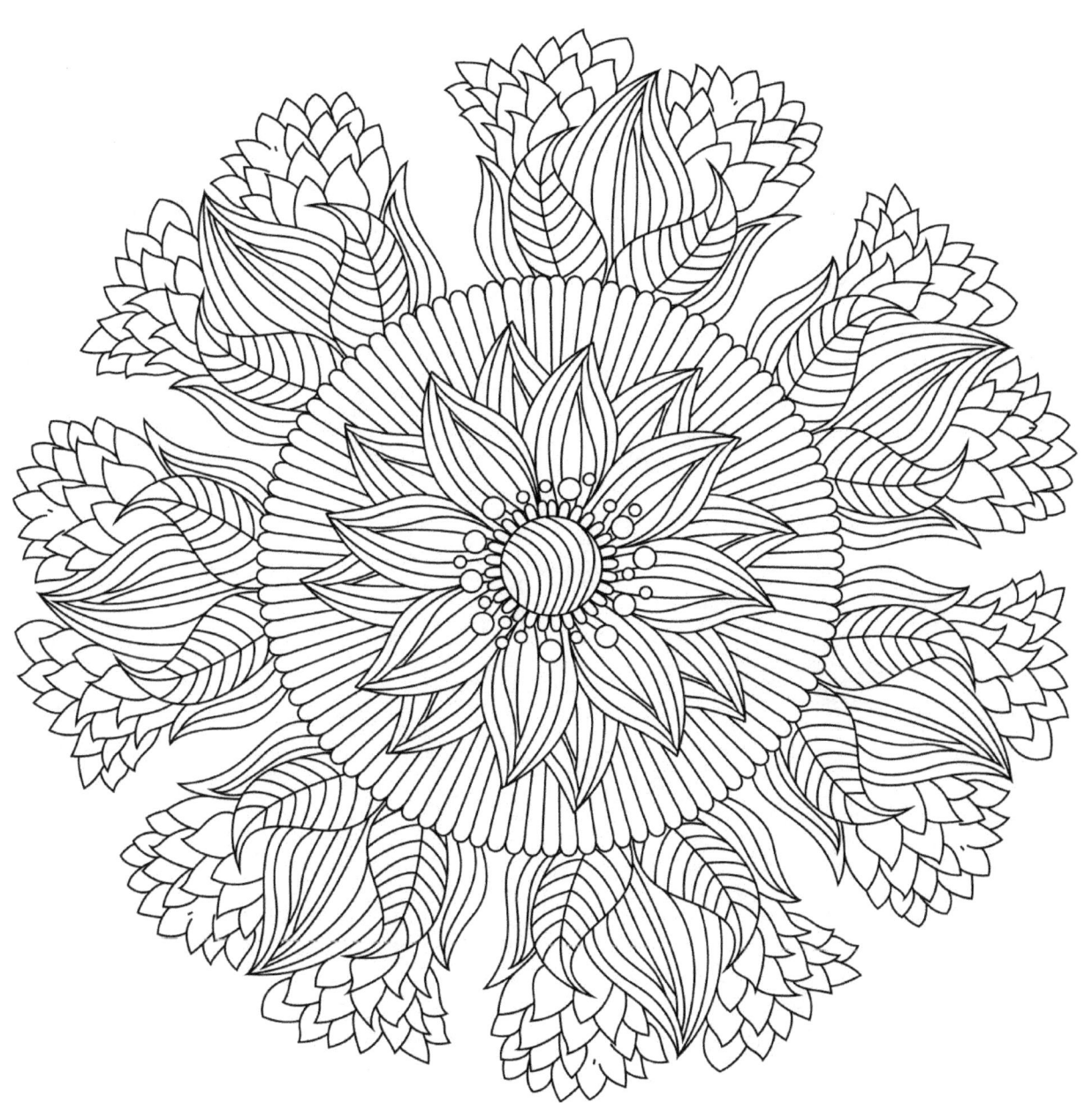

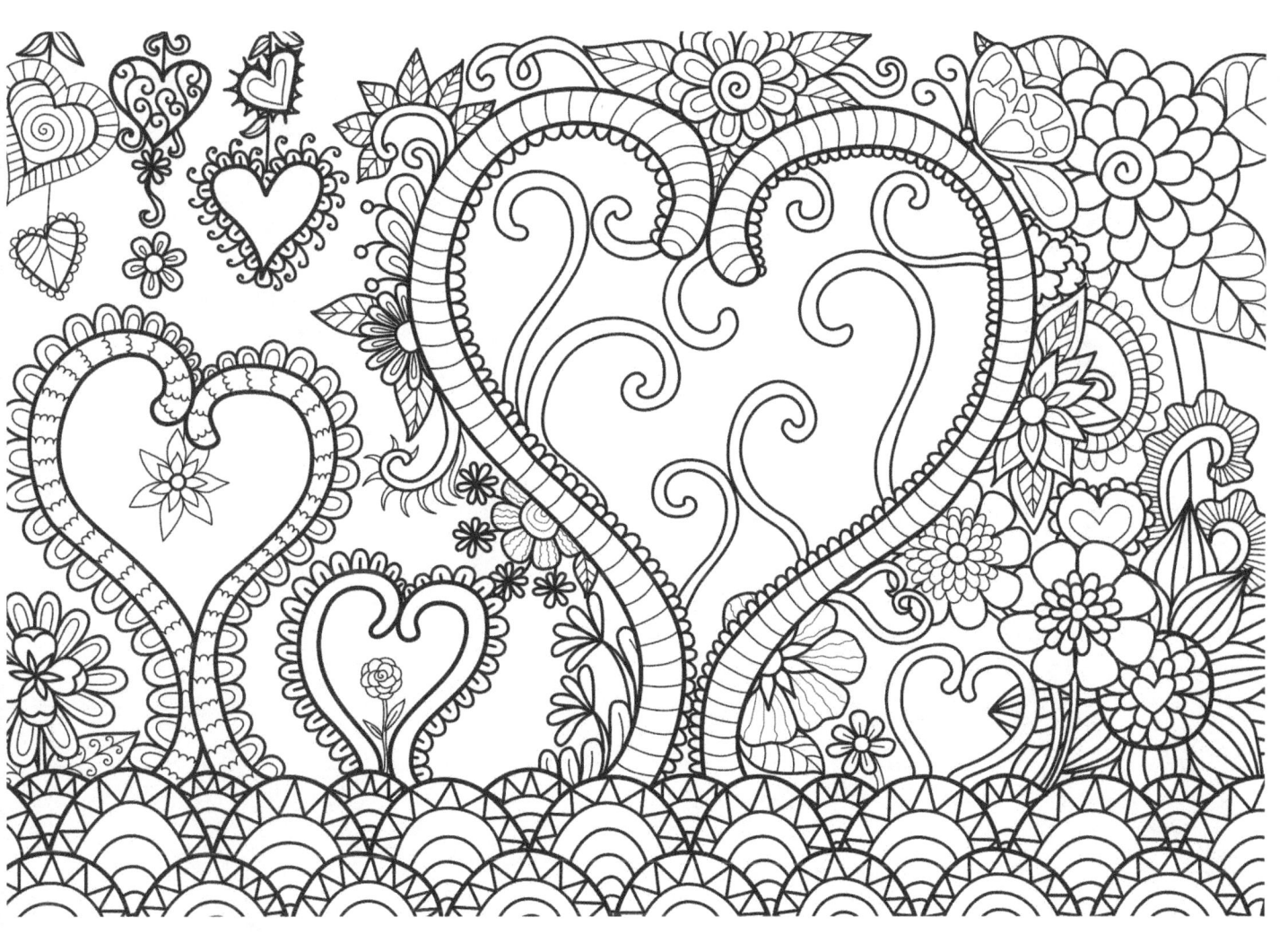

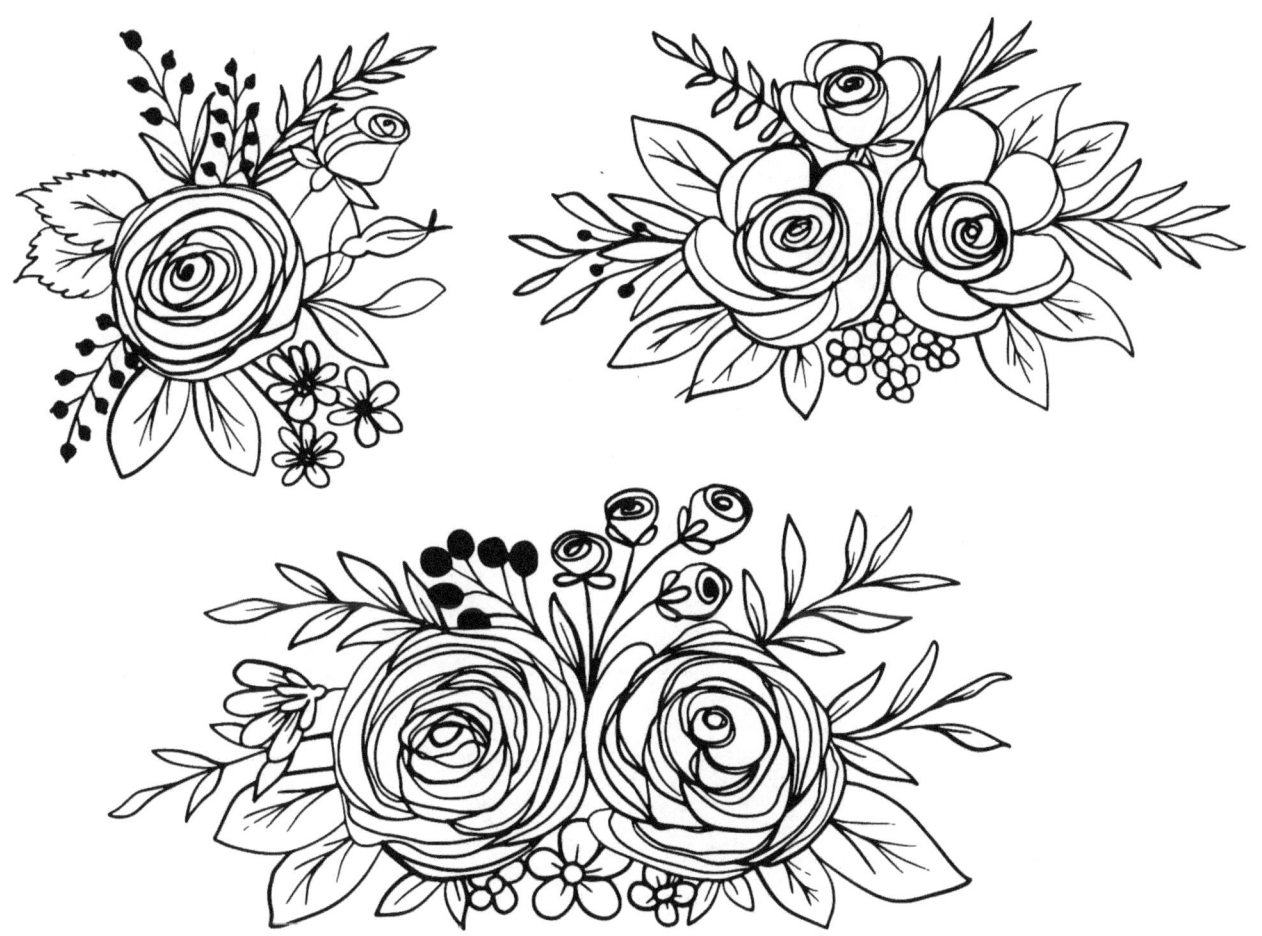

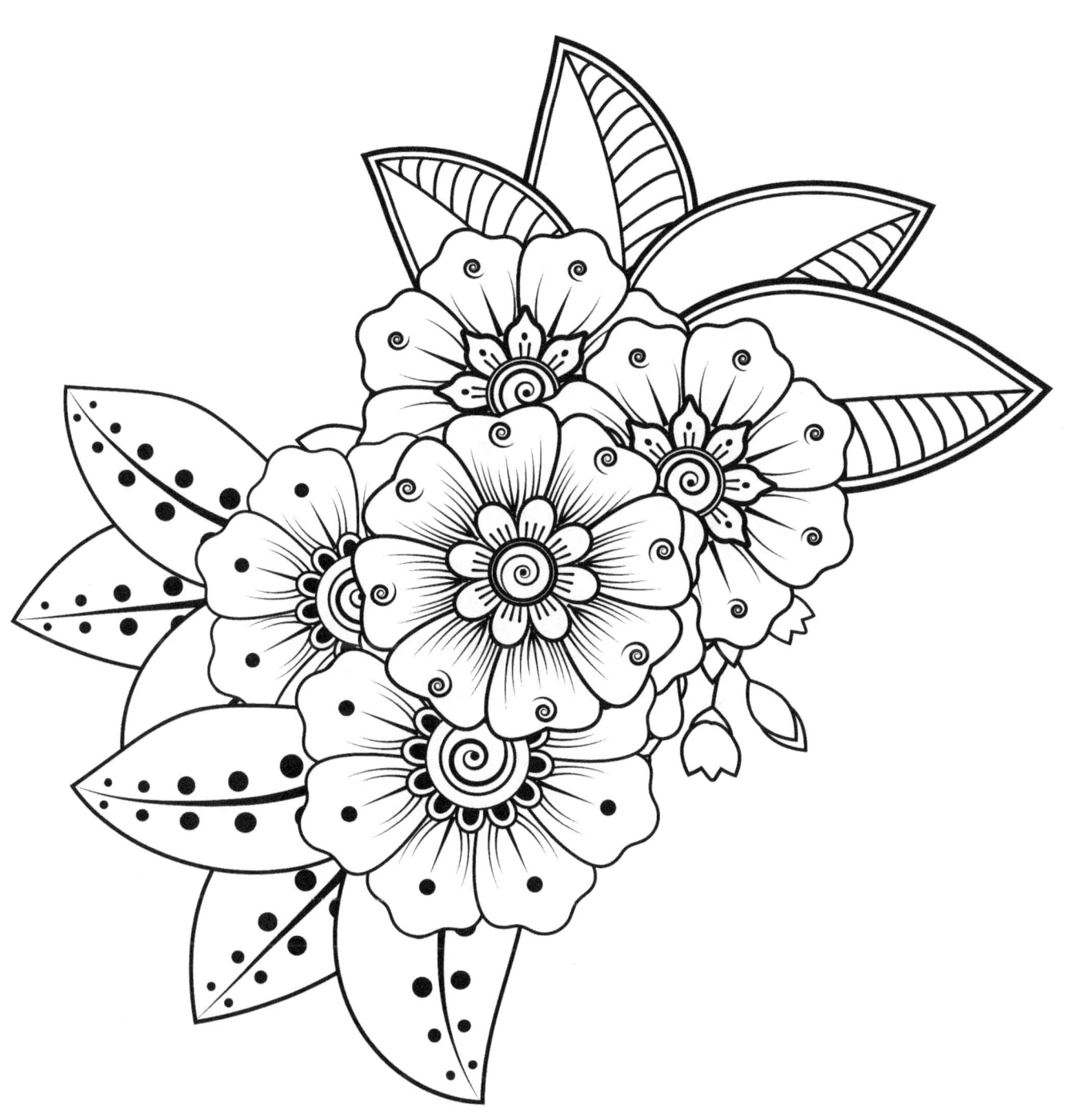

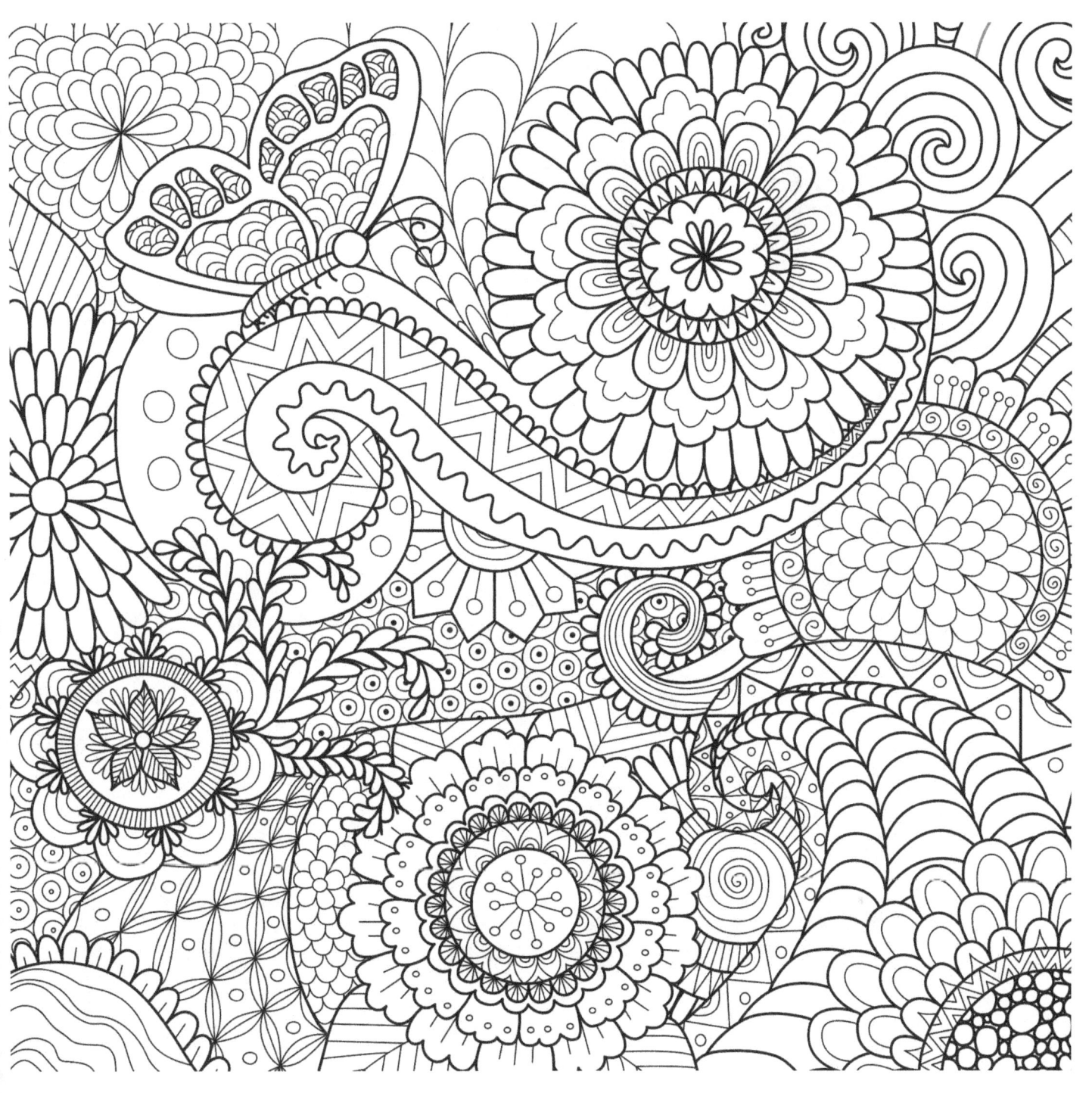

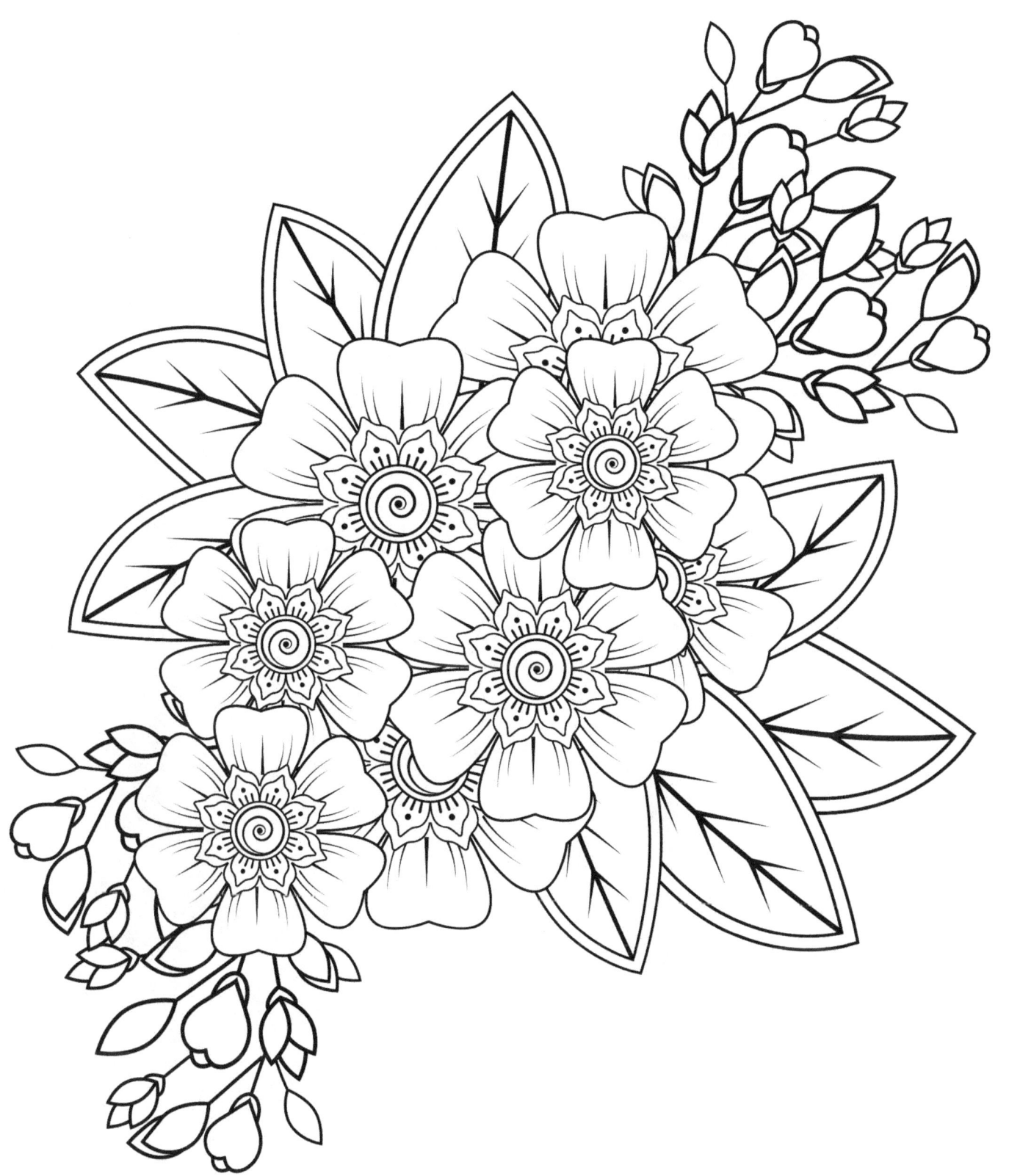

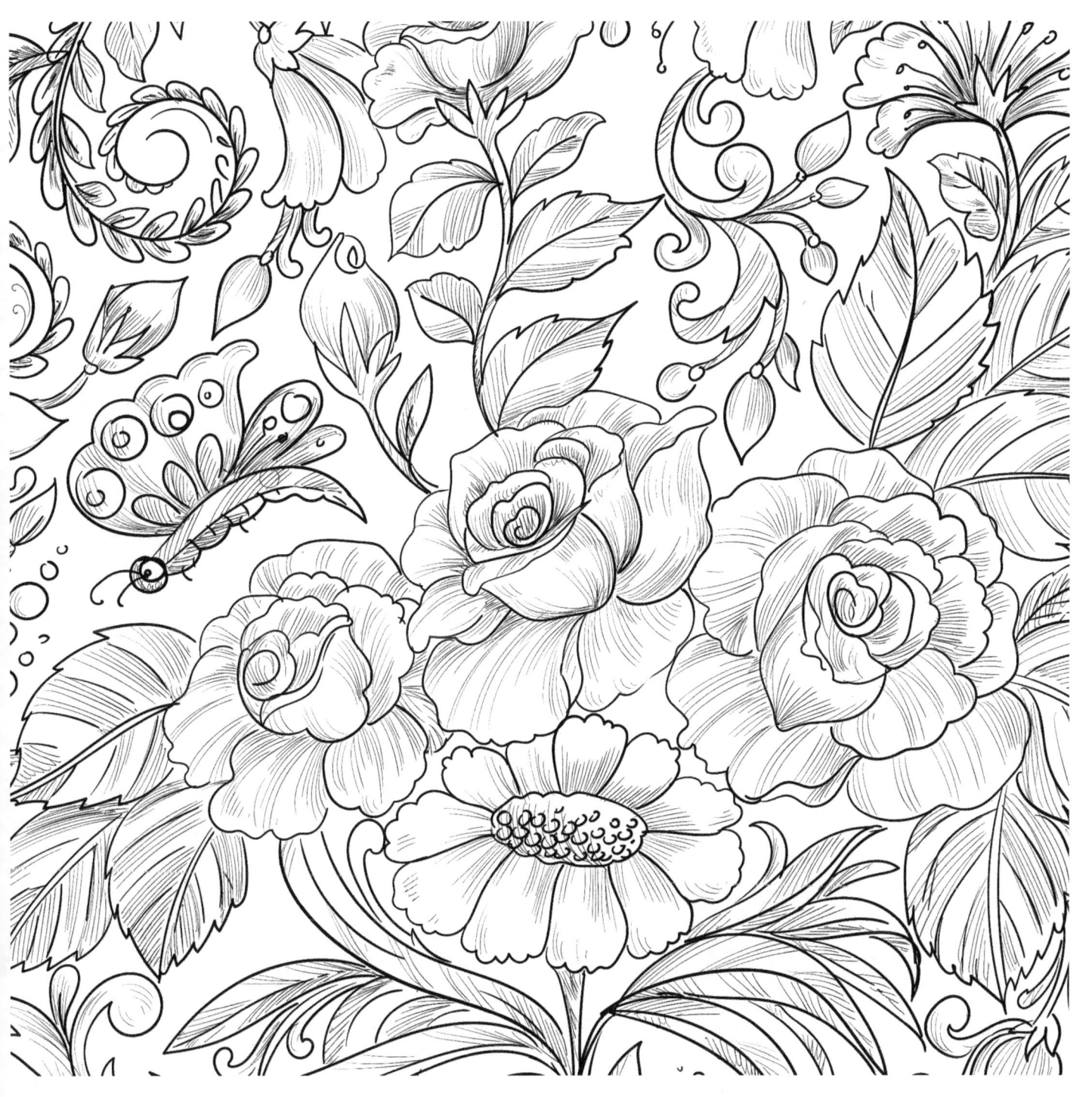

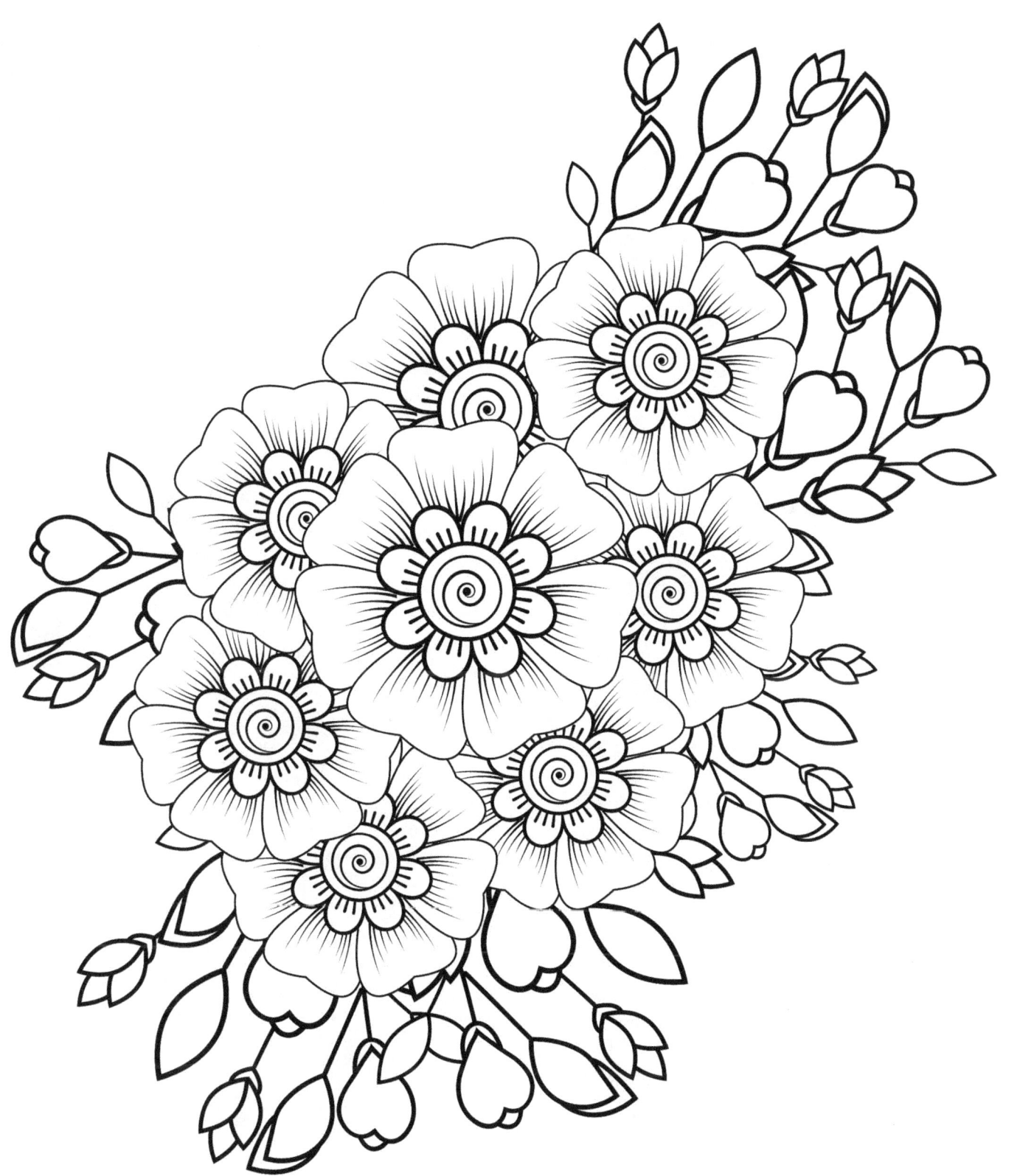

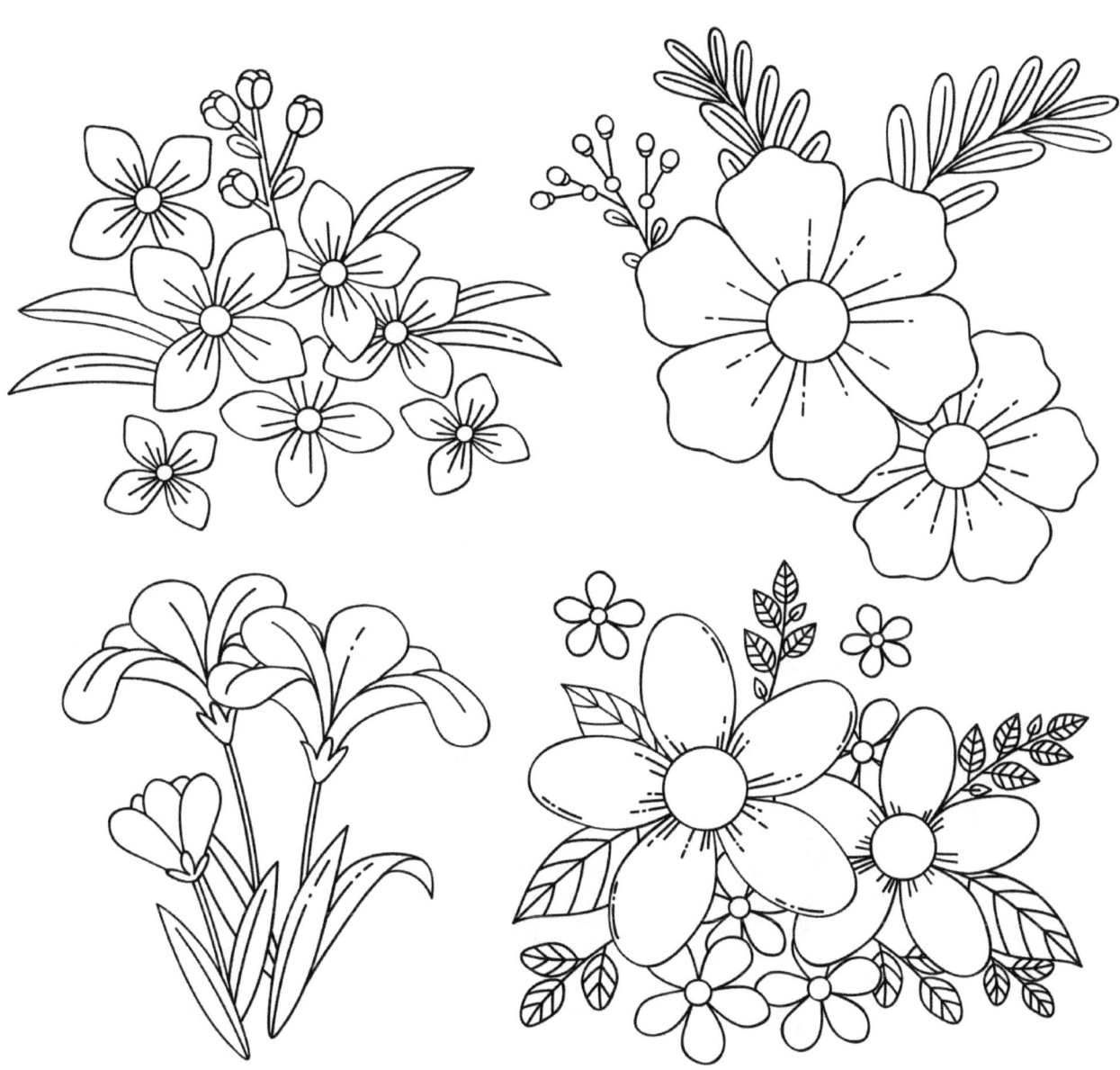

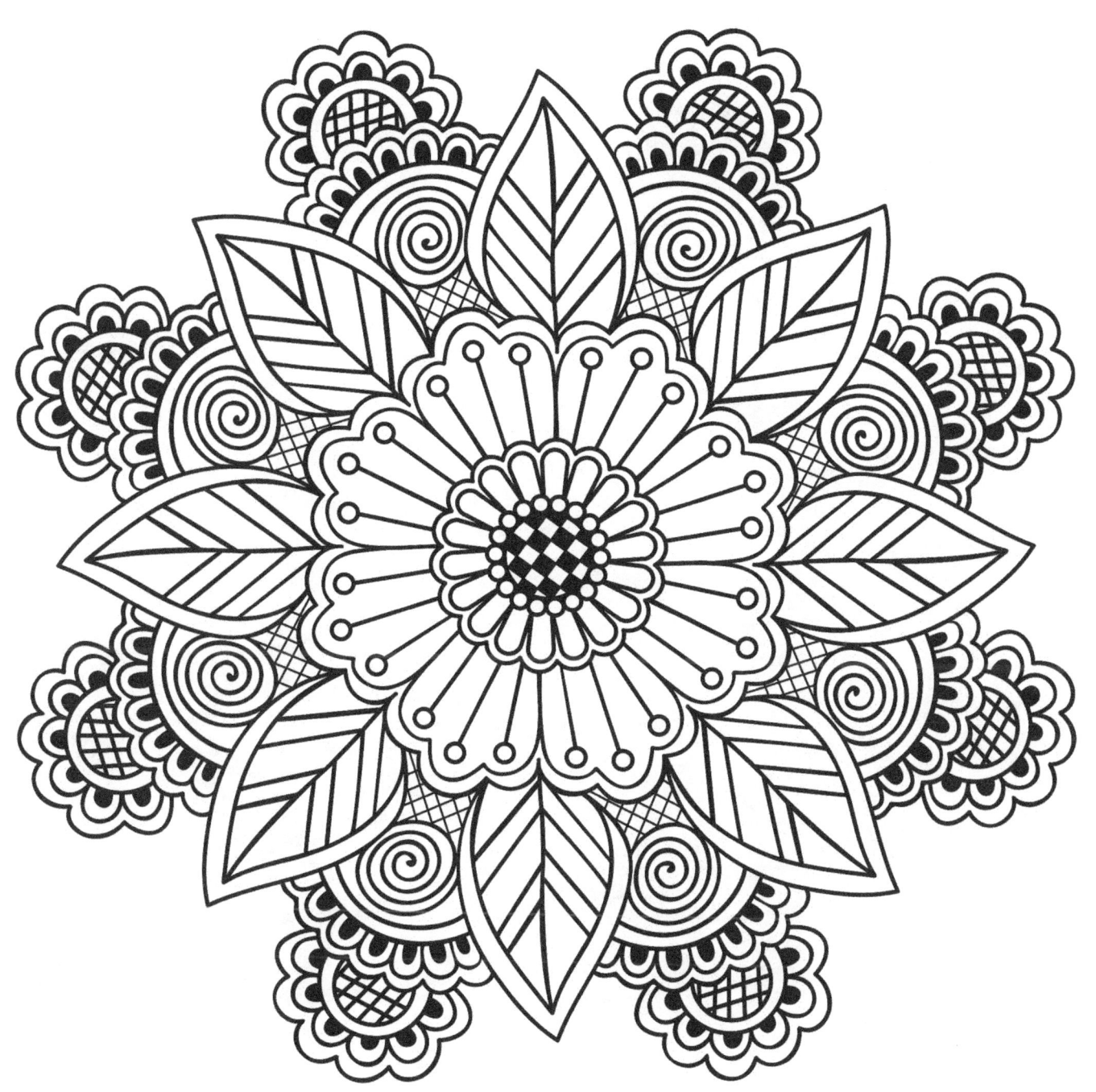

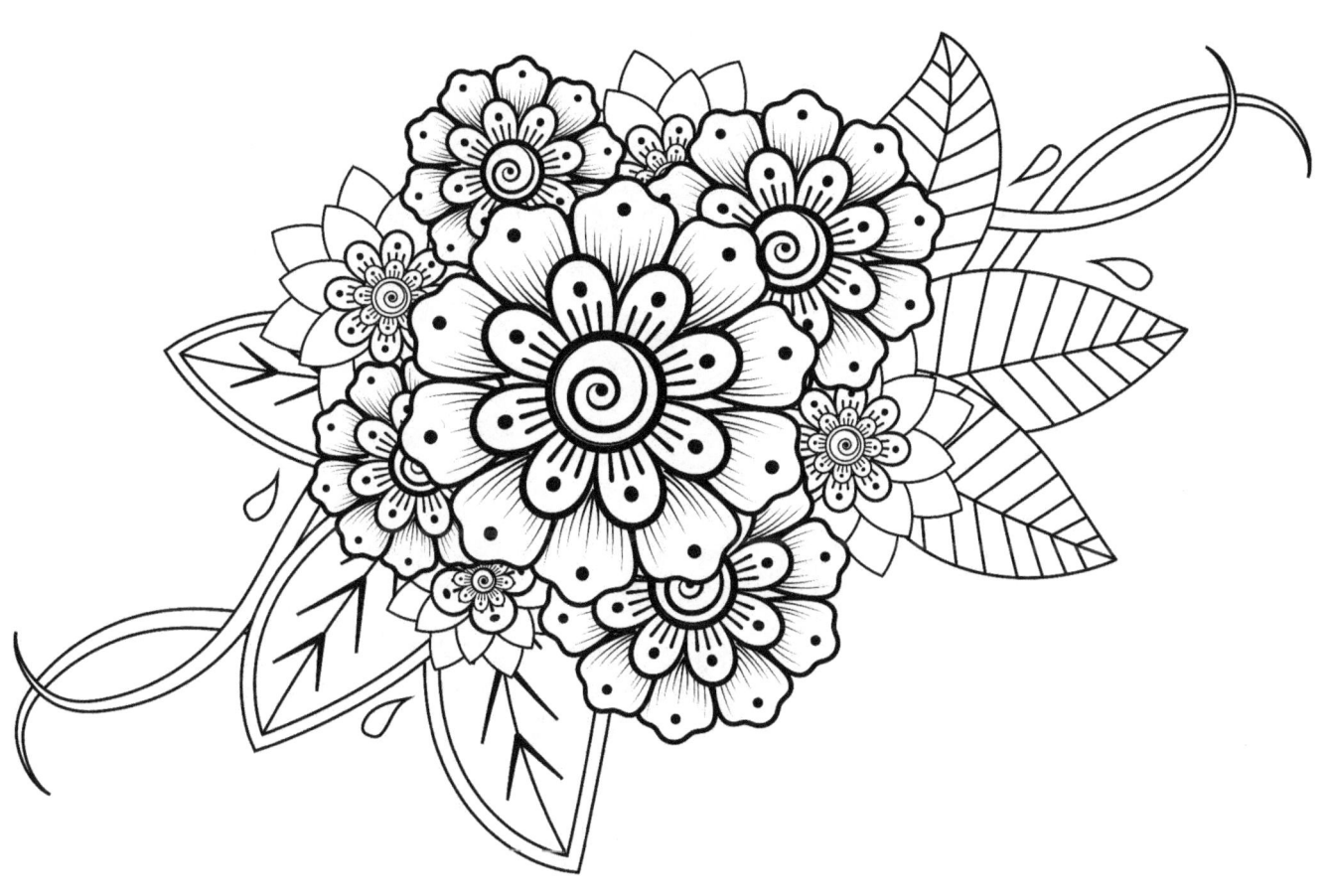

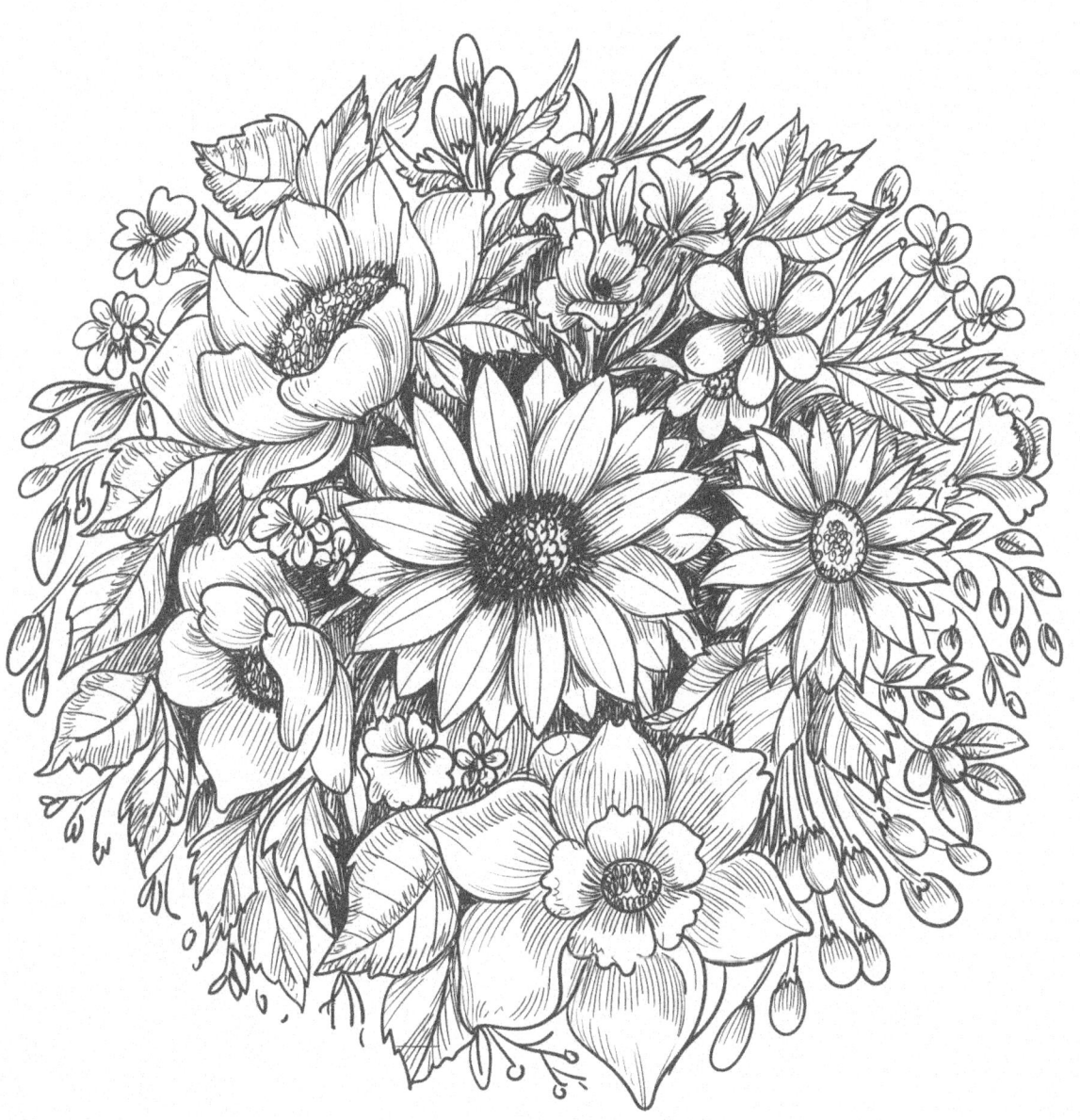

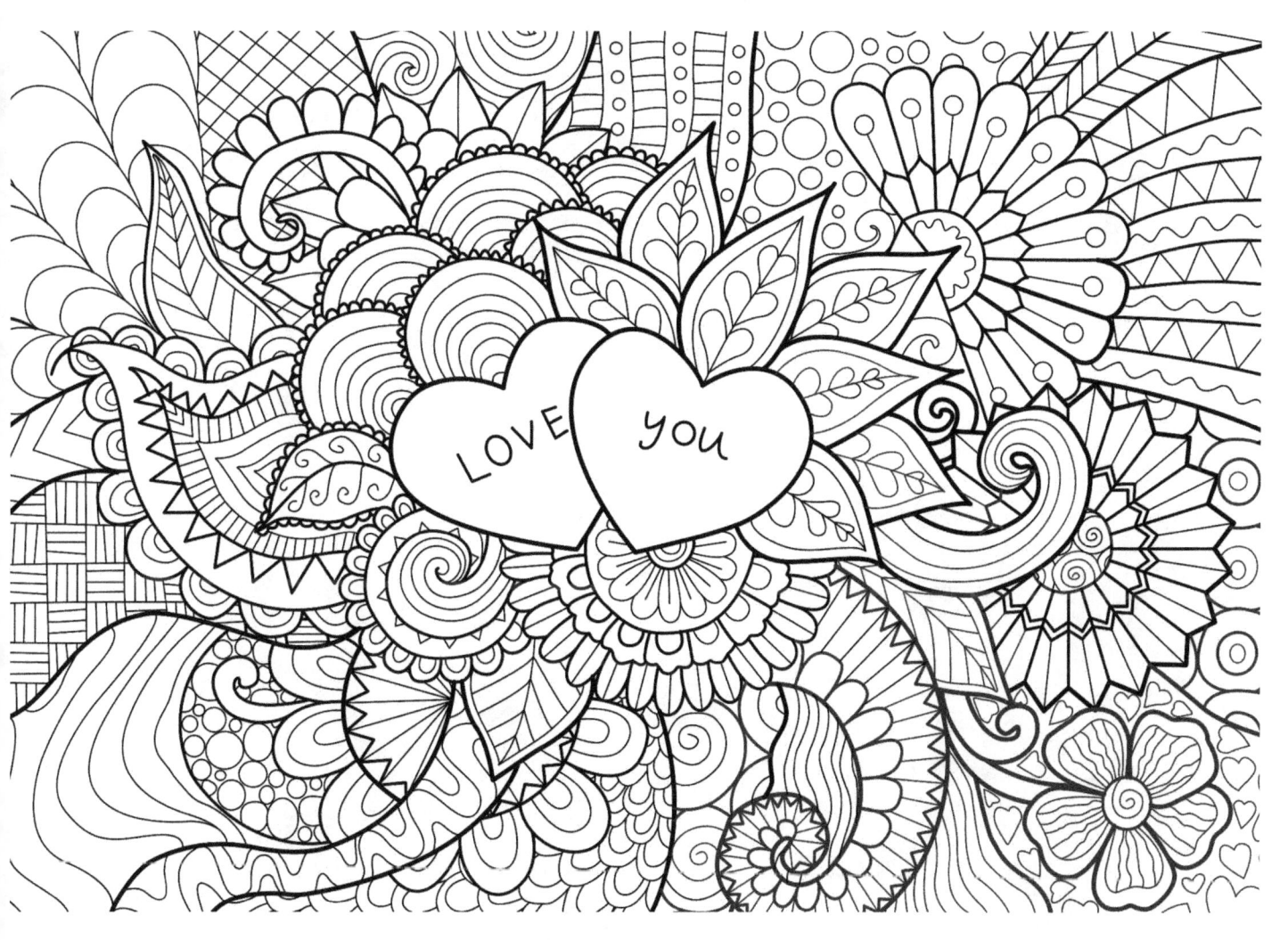

CPSIA information can be obtained
at www.ICGtesting.com
Printed in the USA
BVHW021443120423
662129BV00025B/597

9 798211 399952